The Annals
of
Trawden Forest

by
Fred Bannister M.A., B.Sc.

Landy Publishing
"Acorns",
3 Staining Rise,
Staining, Blackpool
FY3 0BU
Telephone: (0253) 886103

ISBN: 1 872895 11 5

This is a photographic reproduction of the first edition of this book, which was published in Colne in 1922. The photographs did not appear in that edition.

Printed by Galava Printing Company Limited, Nelson, Lancashire

The Annals
of
Trawden Forest

by
Fred Bannister M.A., B.Sc.

Landy Publishing
1992

Preface

Seventy years have gone by since this book was first published. In many ways, much has changed in the area known as the Forest of Trawden, and yet in other ways, little has changed. Author Fred Bannister would still recognise Trawden, Winewall and Wycoller and be at home with the families of his contemporaries.

Researched with meticulous care, this book is pre-eminent amongst the local history books of East Lancashire, and deserves to be republished so that present and succeeding generations can learn of the area's rich history.

The original publication contained some local adverts which have been left out of this edition and replaced by some photographs.

When summarising his book, Fred Bannister said it *"embraced histories of the families, institutions, buildings, industries, customs and traditions of the Trawden district, showing their connection with Colne and neighbourhood."* There should be such a book covering every part of Lancashire - but there isn't.

The publisher's thanks are owed to Fred Bannister's daughters, Freda and Edith, for giving their permission to reprint. They are due also to Dennis Green of Foulridge, a member of the long-established Bannister family, for lending family photographs and giving advice. Also to Bert Hindle of Colne for the use of his photographs and his advice, to Mr and Mrs Jack Greenwood of Colne for the use of a drawing and their advice, and to Peter Wightman and his staff at Colne Library for the use of their photographs.

THE ANNALS

OF

TRAWDEN FOREST.

The Author :

FRED BANNISTER, M.A., B.Sc.

CONTENTS.

	Page
Preface	2

Chapter
1—The Land and its Settlement	5
2—The Disafforestation	10
3—The Common Lands	16
4—Corn Growing and the Old Corn Mill	22
5—The Coal Industry	27
6—The Cotton Weaving Industry	30
7—The Religious Denominations	36
8—Obsolete Customs and Beliefs	50
9—Poets and Poetry	56
10—Place Names and Dialect Words	66
11—Wycollar and the Cunliffes	73
12—The Foulds Family of Trawden Hall	80
13—Public Institutions	94
14—Local Government	99
15—The Woodlands—Conclusion	104

PREFACE.

"Well done, thou grand old Trawden, at the foot of Boulsworth Hill,
Where men have lived, and still do live, possessed of mind and will."

So ran the rhymes of a Colne gentleman about 36 years ago as
he recited his poem at Trawden, attracting my attention, because from
my earliest years I had a lively interest in things historic and antiquarian,
and greatly regretted that no one had ever attempted to record local
events and folk-lore. When people told of old customs and striking
incidents it seemed a pity that no one recorded them permanently for the
instruction and amusement of future generations. Twice I started to
make a contemporary record, but was so disappointed with my efforts
that I destroyed them. At the same time, however, I extracted every
note relating to Trawden which could be found in the various histories
of Lancashire, and also in that treasure of local interest, "The Annals
of Colne." From elderly people I gathered many items of local knowledge and preserved these notes in the hope that at some future time
they might be of value to any local historian or descriptive writer. Had
my native village no history worth recording? Was it ever a great
forest, as its name suggested? When did people first settle there and
who were they? Who originally owned the land and how did it develop
into the present system of small farms? Who first built the stone walls
round the fields? Had the moor ever been common property? Who
first built the farmhouses and gave them names? Why had the story
and romance of Trawden Hall and its owners never been preserved?
Why did we have a characteristic dialect, and lastly why did people in
other places seek laughter and cheap popularity by attaching the name
of Trawden to any ridiculous story they had heard, read, or invented?

Such were the questions that frequently rose in my mind, and
for which I could find no answer.

After twenty years of city life, on returning to live in Colne, it
was my good fortune to meet friends who were able to supplement many
of my earlier notes, and this led to an extensive research of peculiar
interest, although often laborious, and the accumulation of a mass of
material, much of which has never been published. As a contribution
of local history brief outlines of this record were given to The Literary
and Scientific Society of Colne, the town on which Trawden has always
been dependent. In response to the great interest shown, it seemed
appropriate to publish the complete record in the local paper, "The Colne
and Nelson Times."

F. B.

THE ANNALS OF
TRAWDEN FOREST.

CHAPTER I.

THE LAND AND ITS SETTLEMENT.

Trawden Forest extends from the boundaries of Colne, to the south and south-west, over the nearer northern slope of Boulsworth Hill to the farther southern slope, where it forms the county boundary of Lancashire. It has three main divisions, Trawden in the west, Winewall in the centre, and Wycollar in the northeast, each of which extends from the Colne boundary to the Yorkshire border. The county boundary line has an elevation of from 1,500 to 1,000 feet above sea level, and is the termination of the districts of Oakworth, Stanbury, Walshaw, Wadsworth, and Widdop, in Yorkshire, and of Extwistle, Briercliffe, and Nelson in Lancashire. The highest point of Boulsworth Hill, Ladlow Stones, 1,700 feet above sea level, and a considerable area on the top of the moor, lie well within the boundary of Trawden Forest.

The general slope of the land is to the north-west, with two main depressions through which run Trawden brook and Wycollar brook to join Colne water, which was formerly the northern boundary. Winewall lies between the two main streams at the northern end of the township and near the junction of Trawden brook and Colne water. The hamlet of Trawden has always been of greater importance than either of the sister hamlets of Winewall and Wycollar, and it is mainly with Trawden that I shall deal. There is no important highway through the Forest, and this fact has probably led to greater seciusion and a greater development of local character than would otherwise have been the case.

From Colne a road goes up to Wycollar through Winewall, and connects up to the Colne-Haworth highway, and by an old road, Rock Lane, to Trawden. •The other old road leads by Carry Bridge, up Coalpit Lane over the Mirage to Trawden Hill. The modern road, Skipton Road, but always referred to as the "New Road," follows closely the track of Trawden water from its junction with Colne water at Cotton Tree. No record has yet been discovered to indicate which of the three villages is the oldest.

In the first great land survey of England made at the direction of William the Conqueror, and recorded in the Dómesday Book in 1086 A.D., the whole of the lands of this district were recorded as "wastes," and were granted as part of the Hundred of Blackburn to the Norman knight, Roger of Poictou, who built Clitheroe Castle. Robert de Lacy succeeded him, and by the marriage of his only surviving daughter, these lands became and remained a part of the Duchy of Lancaster, until the Restoration of Charles the Second. They were then bestowed on George Monk, the Duke of Albemarle, as a reward for his services to the king, and after his death in 1670 they passed through the House of Montague, to that of the Duke of Buccleuch, and then to the Clitheroe Estates Company.

The earliest record in which Trawden Forest is mentioned is in the Compotus or yearly account presented by the steward at the Manor House of Ightenhill for Henry de Lacy, the Earl of Lincoln, who was then Lord of the Manor. Clitheroe Castle was his Lancashire stronghold and residence lying midway between his other castles of Lancaster and Pontefract. At Colne he had a manor house, and his hunting forests included those of Pendle, Accrington, Rossendale, and Trawden. He also had twenty-nine cattle breeding farms, or vaccaries, one of which was Trochdene. Over the vaccary was a bailiff or Instaurator, and his yearly account of the stock of cattle, the Instauratum, shows that the total stock of cattle numbered 407, in the charge of five assistant cowherds who sheltered in booths. The names of these boothmen are given as Adam, son of John, Matilda wife of Jordan del Bothe, Emma del Munkrode, Henry de Emot, and Peter del Fernyside. The cattle reared were of small size, and oxen were of more value than cows because they were used to draw waggons or ploughs. An ox was then worth 9/-., a cow 7/-, a hide 2/6, while a cart horse cost £2 to £3. The cattle were affected to some extent with the murrain, but they suffered more from the ravages of wolves, which then infested the district. At each booth it is recorded that cattle have been lost by the attacks of wolves. Such a country was not suitable for sheep-farming, and neither sheep nor wool are mentioned.

The first mention of "Wynewelle in Trochdene Forest" occurs in connection with the building anew of one barn there at a cost of £1/2/1½,, and for repairing one house there thrown down by one oak the sum of 3/6 was paid. The wages of a man for guarding calves from the wolf is given as one shilling and twopence.

6

The most interesting item is that "sea-coal" was sold in Trawden for ten shillings in 1296. The coal used in London and in the south of England was called "sea-coal" for centuries, because it was imported by sea from the coal mines of Northumberland and Durham. The earliest official record of coal in Northumberland was in 1234 A.D., when Henry III. granted the men of Newcastle a license to dig coal. The first mention of sea-coal was at Dover in 1278, and yet 18 years afterwards it is recorded as having been sold in Trawden. A probable explanation of this fact is that it was known by that name at Lincoln, and this district being one of the forests of De Lacy, the Earl of Lincoln, the same name was applied to coal here. In 1305 the sea-coal in Trawden yielded sixteen shillings.

These Compoti give us an outline of life in the Forest under the rule of a Norman Earl, when the tenants were few in number and mainly occupied with the rearing of cattle, or winning of sea-coal. As the lands passed by marriage to the Duke of Lancaster, and thence to the King of England, the tenants are referred to as belonging to the reigning King or Queen.

A survey of the manor of Colne in 1323 states that there are five vaccaries in Trouden and that there is greater advantage to the king to adgist or pasture these vaccaries by a suitable number of cows than to set them out to farm. It is also recorded that in this year a band of raiders from Craven and Airedale headed by Nicholas de Mauleverer the Constable of Skipton Castle did take from the cattle breeding establishments a large number of cows and bulls. Trespasses and deer stealing were reported in Trawden as in other forests, and in 1345 William Fauvell and others were charged with having entered Queen Isabella's free chase at Trawden, hunted there, and carried deer away, and assaulted her servant Adam the Procter. There was a conviction with damages assessed at £6/13/4. In 1423, in the Compotus of Henry de Hoghton, the Master Forester of Blackburnshire, the wages of one moor driver at Trouden, watching the animals when they try to stray into Yorkshire, is given as 6d. per week for thirty-one weeks. He was unable to watch the animals there without assistance, so four shillings and twopence was charged for the wages of an attendant. The collectors of the herbage reported that nineteen acres of waste land in Trouden were demised to Lawrence Parker at fourpence per acre, that winter herbage yielded nothing, because in the chase the grass is consumed by the King's animals, and from the grass sown for mowing there

7

is no revenue because it is reserved for the King's wild animals. The master forester was named William Nutter, and his wages were twopence per day. Not content with the ordinary revenue from his forests, the money-loving king, Henry VII., sent a Commission to revive Puture Rents, which will be understood from the following statement :—
"Whereas of old use and custom the foresters and keepers of our Forests of Pendle, Rossendale, Accrington, and Trawden have had of very right and duty at certain times and days, meat and drink of the tenants therein and adjoining, the which is now called Puture or Forester Fee, it also appeareth that for divers displeasures and annoyances that the said Foresters committed against the tenants, their wives and servants, the tenants made complaint to our progenitors, Dukes of Lancaster, and bound themselves to pay for the time being £12/13/4 to the said Foresters towards their wages, and in recompence of meat and drink called Forester Fee, which was paid to the first year of Edward IV., then the said Puture was put in respite so that £119/6/8 is now in respite which if it should be longer delayed would turn to our disinheritance and the utter destruction of our Foresters for lack of keeping. Wherefore enquire which tenants ought to pay the said duties, and what everyone of them after the old usage and custom there, and thereupon compel them to pay it, or distrain them and for utter refusing seize on their tenures immediately, and admit such other persons as will be content to pay the said duties."

These extracts give us a picture of the earliest recorded settlements in the district. There were a few vaccaries rearing cattle for the lord of the manor, the king or queen, while the greater part of the land formed a deer forest, in which there were also wolves and wild boars. Throughout the 15th century the system of vaccaries seems to have continued, but there would be a gradual breaking up of the forest land and an influx of people until the disafforestation in 1506. In 1423, the Forest of Trawden contained five vaccaries, viz., Over and Nether Wycoller, Wynewall, and Over and Nether Beardshaw. For many years after this date, the name Trawden is used for the Forest only and not for the village or vaccary. The names Over and Nether Beardshaw are used to signify the residential part of Trawden. It is of interest to notice that the names of Beardshaw and Beardshawhead still remain as the names of farms overlooking the Cathole Clough.

The yearly value of the vaccaries increased from £2/8/- in 1323, when they were managed by herders or boothmen, to £21/13/4 in 1423.

8

The system had then changed, and the vaccaries were let out to the highest bidder, on short leases of seven or ten years. In 1478, Lord Stanley leased Beardshaw Booth, and in 1503, the Earl of Derby and James Stanley, his son, leased all the vaccaries for twenty-one years, the lessees to repair all buildings.

The civil court before which disputes were settled was called the Woodmote. This was probably held at the same time and place as the Halmote of the manor of Colne. Fines derived from pleas of debt or trespass amounted to 3/- in 1423 and 6/9 in 1443.

CHAPTER II.
THE DISAFFORESTATION.

It has been previously described how the system of direct cattle farming had been replaced by a system of short leases, at the end of the 15th century. A great change occurred in 1506, when Royal Commissioners surveyed, partitioned, and let the five vaccaries which were included in Trawden Forest to divers tenants who occupied holdings extending altogether to 2,818 acres, or about one-third of the total area of the Forest. These holdings were the origin of the present system of farms, and many of the place names have continued without appreciable change during the last 400 years. This breaking up of the King's forest into a system of small farms and cottages was called the disafforestation.

Up to 1506 it was a forest used for cattle rearing and for the hunting of wild beasts, a forest not completely covered with trees, although there were many more trees than there are at present, but it consisted largely of grassland. New farms were gradually made by cultivating the waste forest land, but a large amount of common land remained on which the different tenants could pasture their cattle. No tenant however could send as many cattle as he pleased to the common, but only a certain number in proportion to the extent of his holding. Frequently there were disputes because tenants had sent more cattle to the common land than they were entitled to, or the cattle had trespassed, or new fences had been erected or old fences had been broken down.

The court of law to settle such disputes was formed by the inhabitants among themselves. The people were mutually responsible for the maintenance of law and order. The law was not a written one, but the ancient custom of the people as declared to be true by a jury of twelve of the oldest inhabitants. One can readily see that such a meeting would always be an enquiry to decide what had been the immemorial custom of the township, and thus it was always called an inquest or inquisition. This system was a survival of a very ancient Anglo-Saxon custom, and the ancient word, mote or moot, which means a meeting, was always used for it. When it was held in the woods it was a Woodmote, a name already used in this history. If held at the hall of the lord of the manor, it was a Hallmote, or Halmot as it is called to-day, for jurors are still called half-yearly to the Halmot Court to hold an Inquisition and see that ancient customs are kept. Similarly the meeting for shire or county was the Shiremoot, and the meeting place, as in the city of Durham, is still called the Moothall.

At the head of the Inquisition was the Greave, the chief officer of the township, elected by the tenants from among those of their own number having most substance and ability. Each tenant was liable for this service, which seems originally to have been held for one year only. There was also a Constable or Pinner, who was elected to seize cattle trespassing or wandering at large, or to take them in distraint for debt, and lodge them in the village pinfold, there to be kept until they were redeemed by the owner on payment of a fine. An Affeeror was appointed to settle fines imposed for breaches of well-known village customs, which were first called byre-laws, from which we get our modern word bye-laws. The Fencelooker had an important office in those days, when fences were first erected and the common lands and enclosed lands were so similar. The Aletaster had a peculiar occupation, but there is no record during the next century that he made any complaint.

The rent payable was fourpence per Lancashire acre of twenty yards to the perch, and a fine of one year's rent was payable on admittance to a holding. The Hallmoot or Halmot Court was the meeting of the tenants, and was concerned only with the lands which had never been granted out or sublet under the Feudal System, but had remained a part of the lord's manor which in this case was the Honor of Clitheroe. Each tenant held his lands directly from his lord by a copy of the Court Roll without any intermediary. He was thus a copyholder, his land was called copyhold, and his rent, copyhold rent. This system has survived, but while the copyhold rents have never altered, the value in buildings and improvements have continuously appreciated, so that now the copyhold rent, or "Duke's rent" as it is frequently called, is very small in comparison with the ordinary rent which a tenant is willing to give for any property he desires to hold himself or to sublet in the Forest. Even now, however, any owner must be willing to render suit and service at the Halmot Court to the lord of the manor, the vendor must surrender his land or buildings to the lord of the manor, while the purchaser receives them back from that source. If the landlord dies without heir his property reverts to the original landlord, the lord of the manor.

The first Inquisition of the Forest of Trawden was held in May, 1510, by the oath of fourteen tenants, nine of whom had the surname of Hartley, one of Shotilworth, one Smyth, two of Shakylton, and one Driver. If we could trace out the history of a single family in some detail it would provide an invaluable record and description of these distant times. The Hartleys have always predominated in number, and for long after this date they were probably most important, but having no distinguishing marks of family or place of abode, it is impossible to trace a regular sequence in their holdings. The only family of importance of which any record of succession over a considerable period of time can be attempted, is that of the Foldes and Pillings of Trawden House. In a later section this will be given.

At the Halmot Court of 1510 there is a complaint that the tenants of Trawden have obstructed the high road between Emmut Brigge (Laneshawbridge) and Sholfolt (Shelfield), and they are warned to repair it before the ensuing feast of the Nativity of St. John the Baptist, on pain of a penalty of 6/8.

John Hartley surrendered one messuage and all buildings with appurtenances in Beardshaw Booth, of the yearly rent of twenty shillings, to Thomas Emmott, Henry Shagh, Henry Walton, and John Hanson.

Henry Walton was fined two shillings for breaking the King's fold in Trawden.

There were many fines of 2d., 3d. or 4d. each for trespassing, and 3d. for keeping open fences; in fact this seems to have formed the chief business of the jury. It is interesting to note that the total fines at this time for Trawden were much higher than those for Colne. In six successive courts the yields are for Colne, 2/2, 4/11, 6/10, 15/3, 3/4, and 6/2, and for Trawden, 7/2, 9/7, 14/5, 29/7, 62/8, 90/8.

In 1515, Robert Blakey complains against Henry Walton, of Marsden, for taking away a horse, also against John the Abbot of Whalley for treading down his corn and grass with his beasts, also against John Bakster and Katrine his wife in a plea of debt for 13d., being plaintiff's charge for teaching.

A chantry priest, William Hird, is mentioned in 1516. There is no record of the bequest which supported this man, but there is a Latin inscription carved in oak, a prayer addressed to the Virgin, by William Hyrd, on the wall of the north chancel of Colne Parish Church.

In 1522 four hedge-lookers, all with the surname of Hartley, were appointed to supervise the setting out of new hedges and to apportion the making and repairing of the same between the various occupiers of the land to be fenced. This must have been a period of great activity owing to the subdivision of the Forest into many holdings, with a large amount of hedging and fencing, requiring the services of surveyors or supervisors. Opposition was shown to this active enclosure, for in 1529, several tenants of Beardshaw Booth complain against others for unjust occupation of land, Whittley house and other lands on the south side, and of all buildings lately built there, to the injury of the tenants who had lately made fine for land taken from the King's waste as appears by the Rolls to their injury in the sum of £10. A priest, Nicholas Hartley, is ordered to leave a highway for all tenants coming and going with their carts. Also all buildings, crofts, and gardens, now existing, enclosed, encroached, built, or situate within Beardshaw Booth shall be measured, and each shall have a portion of such messuages, gardens, and crofts, according to the rate and quantity of the rent of each tenant. The tenants shall have a way, nine feet wide, to the common pasture, and if they lack sufficient allotment there, as they justly should have, then they shall enclose as much measurement in the Cowclose and Oxclose as they shall lack, as near their houses, barns, and gardens as possible. Further, if any tenants shall not have houses, barns or gardens, it shall be allowed to each to enclose and encroach as much as he may lack up to the next "le alez" (occupation road). The allotment was made by the award of the Steward and with the help of an instrument, called in the Roll "the metter of land," probably a rod or ash pole cut to a length exactly proportionate to the amount of copyhold rent payable for the holding, each tenant having his own "metter," wherewith his allotment of ground, meadows, and common pastures could be accurately measured, set out and awarded.

There were no proper roads in those days, but simply field tracks with rights of way. It is not surprising, therefore, that complaints should frequently arise because tenants tried to stop these roads. In 1532, Geoffrey Folds, Greave of Trawden, complained of trespass against John and James Herteley for destroying and ploughing his field way so that he could not cross to his land. The Jury declared that the defendants should at their own expense make a sufficient way and that they should not plough the said way from "le marege howse" as far as the high road on the eastern side of the said "marege howse."

In 1540, at the Colne Halmot, the King's tenants of Wycoller and Wynewall claimed a right of way "Through Carre Hey from the east side of Carre Hey Holme, descending downe on the Southe syde of the water unto the yait at the west end within too roode for horse and man, and horse with pack and loyde. Also a Hyeway for cart and wane horse and loyde ever moore to be laid from the Carre Hey to the Wynewall Brig ende upon the lands of John Ruscheworthe. And from the Wynewall Brig ende through the East part of a Holme of Richard Towneley caled Mithome Holme heid and from there through Danbanke on Sclanatt Shoryng, and compassyng the Browe to Ricroft Feild Syde to the Moore called Lee Moore.''

In another case a farmer was declared to have the right to drive his cattle three times a year across the defendant's land.

In 1534, a letter from Henry VIII. announced that there must be no further division of estates into small "quillets," but that the yearly value of each tenement must be at least 26/8 above all other charges.

In 1538 Carre Heyez (Carry Heys) is stated to be in the Forest of Trawden of ancient tenure, showing that the division between Colne and Trawden then followed the course of the river at Colne Waterside. The name "Carr" means a marsh or marshy place, and Carry Heys, "the edge of the marshy place," which is probably a description of the flood plain that now lies between Carry Bridge and Cottontree. Black Carr and Whiteley Carr in the Trawden valley were exactly similar places.

In the third year of the reign of Philip and Mary, 1557, a complaint was made that Roger Gartside, gentleman, by a commission of their Majesties took three acres of land lying in the Forest of Trawden, to wit, one acre in Logeholme, one acre in Yelloholme, one acre in Nettil hill adjoining to one another. One of the tenants, James Hartley, came forward with a writ of "supersedias," for excusing and forbearing the customary fine. The recital of the full titles of their Majesties in this document is interesting. It begins, "To our trusty and well beloved Sir Thomas Talbot, steward of our hundred of Blackburnshire.''

"Philip and Mary, by the grace of God, King and Queen of England, Spain, France, both Sicilies, Jerusalem and Ireland, Defender of the Faith, Archdukes of Burgundy, Milan, and Brabant, Counties of Haspurge, Flanders, and Tyrol.''

The document states that although lately letters were sent assigning three acres of land within our Forest of Trawden to Roger Gartside under a yearly rent of 4d. per acre, James Hertly hath shown faire copies of a commission in the time of Henry VII. authorising him to let by copy of Court Roll the said three acres and other lands, wherefore for divers considerations us moving hereof, you do not in any way proceed to the execution of the tenor of our former letters concerning these three acres. And these our letters shall be your sufficient warrant and discharge in this behalf.

From the preceding references to complaints and fines, it must not be supposed that such complaints, disputes, trespasses, and law-breaking were uncommonly numerous. Frequently there were no complaints at all, and the only record given is, "All things are well within the Forest of Trawden when the Inquisition is taken." This, of course, represented an ideal state of affairs, but it is barren of ideas to the historian who finds in the records of disputes, the names of the inhabitants, the names of their dwellings, and many of their customs, a wealth of information that otherwise would have been forgotten long ago.

CHAPTER III.
THE COMMON LANDS OF TRAWDEN FOREST.

In the middle of the 16th century, each tenant had his homestead with land enclosed near to it, and the right to send a certain number of cattle to the common pastures. Some of these commons can still be located by the names of farms which have taken their place, but most of them have lost their identity during the process of gradual enclosure and cultivation.

In the early Court Rolls, Wicolar Deyne Common and Wynewall Hey Common were frequently named, because people were fined for sending too many cattle to pasture thereon. In a similar way the "Inpasture," the "Owthpasture," and the "Styrkepasture" were mentioned. We cannot tell where these pastures were, but the common pastures of Alderhurst, The Rings, and Shelfield would obviously be near the farms with those names, and these positions show that the common land existed in various parts of the Forest for the greater convenience of the several tenants.

To live peaceably and justly it was essential that every tenant should observe the common byelaws, made for the common welfare, and that neither carelessness nor guilt should go unpunished. Hence the frequent fines for keeping open gaps, for insufficient fences, for trespassing with cattle and so on. One tenant was fined for sending his beasts to the common pasture in winter time, to the injury of his neighbours, while another was declared to be an unreasonable tenant who depastured his cattle by night upon his neighbours' grass. Tenants holding land adjoining the water courses, with a right to the middle of the stream, frequently complained that the water course was being diverted, and claimed its restoration to its ancient channel.

Local rivalry between the different divisions of the Forest has always been a prominent characteristic feature. In 1535, there was a dispute on a large scale between the tenants of Wycollar and those of Winewall. At the Halmote of that year, "John Herteley, John Hanson, Christopher Herteley, Peter Herteley, John Ffolds, and John Emott, tenants of the King in Wynewall, together complain against Roger Herteley of Wynewall, John Herteley sen., John Herteley jun., Hugh Shottylworth, Roger Robert, James Dryver, jun., and James Dryver, sen., tenants of the King in Wycoler, concerning two hundred acres of land, meadow, pasture, feeding ground and moss, lying in Wycoler, belonging to the said plaintiffs, and which the defendants now occupy, enclose, and encroach to their own use, whence they have suffered injury in the sum of £10. The defendants deny the charge, and declare that after there had been discord between them, an agreement had been made and sworn upon God's Holy Evangelists; and afterwards the plaintiffs forgot that they were bound by oath, as well as by the arbitration of Roger Herteley, of Wynewall, sen., John Emott, William Michell, of Colne, and Roger Herteley, of Trawden, as by the arbitration of Christopher Lyster, Esq., upon the occupation, partition, and demise of all the said parties lying in Wicoler and Wynewall, now in litigation between them. Wherefore at this Halmote 24 men from the Forests of Trawden, Penhull, and Rossendale were sworn upon an inquest; but they thereupon declared nothing because the plaintiffs did not pursue their plea."

Enclosures of small portions of land, or "quillets," must have been of frequent occurrence, without the knowledge or consent of the Lord of the Manor, who wished to avoid the creation of a poor and needy population. In 1537, William Herteley, of Trawden, occupied a parcel of land beyond the bounds of the Dooles, and his occupation was agreed to by a special jury. In 1560, James Herteley and Katherine his wife, and Marjary Herteley, widow, complained against Margaret Ffoldes, widow, "for wrongful detention of four beastgates in the oxe-pasture of Trowdene," and claimed £6 damages. The jury say that defendant wrongfully occupied and detained "halffe a beaste gate in le oxe-pasture de Trowdene."

In 1561, James Herteley and other tenants of Trawden obtained a verdict for the partition of lands, tenements, pastures, and moss called tent oxe pasture, in Trawden, against Geoffrey Ffoldes, the defendant.

In 1563, the jury say that no tenants of the Queen's in Trawden shall keep any beasts beyond those now existing under pain of 3/4, also that a pain of 12d. is laid that no tenant put any horse or mare in the Dungydyng, the Rynges, Rengbank, or Allderhirst; that every tenant shall repair his share of hedges and ditches two days after warning be given, under pain of forfeiting 12d. for each "gappe," that the Queen's tenants in Wynewall make and maintain their hedges in the lane and around the Ynges from time to time under pain of 3/4 for each default to be levied to the Queen's use from their goods and chattels and that Thomas Allason and James Emotte fished with a net, contrary to the Statute.

The last sentence shows that fish were more abundant in the waters of the district, and of more value than they are now. There were probably several fishponds, or meres, in this locality, which have since been drained or filled. A complaint was made in 1557 that a certain mere fixed at a place called Sowthill had been taken up and destroyed. There was an interesting byelaw which stated that, "No man ought to fish with any Net or Engine, angling only excepted, but with such Net or Trannel as every mesh shall be two inches and a half wide, except nets only to take Loches, Mennas, Bulheads, Gudgions, Eeles, and none other fish upon pain of twenty shillings for each time offending and loss of the fish and unlawful net." If fish were brought to market, they had to be good and wholesome, and sold at reasonable prices, without excessive gains, for every twelve pence bestowing one penny clear gain over and above their charges.

In 1564, Thomas Emotte was admitted to two messuages, 66 acres of rodeland, and one penny and three pence rent of new improvement $5\frac{1}{2}$ acres of forest land called Emott lying in Colne and in the Forest of Trawden; $18\frac{1}{2}$ acres and a farthing of rodeland together with one messuage built upon the said land and lying in Colne, and two acres and three roods of forest land, lying in Trawden Forest.

The Commission of 1507 authorised the steward to make grants of land by copy of Court Roll. The tenants became owners of the copyholds and held their properties on the titles based on these grounds. Houses and farmsteads were erected. Lands were cleared, drained, manured, tilled, and gradually became much enhanced in value. Sales were negotiated on these titles, and children succeeded as heirs to the various estates, unquestioned. Then the Crown lawyers of James I., in 1607, pretended to discover that these titles were faulty, and that the improved lands were only essart-lands which could not be claimed by the copyholders, and that the occupants were tenants only by sufferance. This destroyed the hopes and comforts of many families throughout the Honor of Clitheroe, who lived in competence and quiet on these new improvements. A lengthened litigation followed. It was a barefaced attempt to extort money on false pretences. The wealthier owners made some commutation, the smaller owners resisted paying their share, thereby showing a sturdy independence. The result was that in 1610 there was passed, "An Act for the perfect creation and confirmation of certain copyhold lands in the honor, castle, manor, and lordship of Clitheroe." The sum to be paid was £3,763, equal to 12 years' ancient rent, but this was afterwards increased to 40 years' rent. A first instalment was paid to James I., a second paid about 1650 was granted by King Charles I. to the Navy and Tower Creditors towards satisfaction of debts contracted in victualling the Navy and Tower. There was a heavy penalty for delay, and the Creditors were severe in levying the money, so those who were careful in preserving their estates procured and paid the whole moiety, with a great overplus amounting to £5,833 in all, and so freed themselves and several others who had no security for confirmation of their customs and estates.

The Copyholders therefore petitioned for power to levy money in arrears and reimburse those who had laid out above their proportion, and that the said Decrees and Customs might be confirmed.

An Act of Confirmation was therefore passed, and on this foundation rests all the titles to copyhold lands in Blackburnshire. By this Act the forests were attached to the adjoining manors, Trawden Forest to Colne, Pendle Forest to Ightenhill, and Rossendale Forest to Accrington.

I have no record of the allocation of the common lands of Trawden, Winewall, and Wycollar, mentioned above. They will probably be given in detail in the Court Rolls preserved in Clitheroe Castle.

The last enclosure of common lands on Boulsworth Hill, which was by far the greatest enclosure, so far as area is concerned, took place in 1821. Full particulars of this are available. Thomas Gee, of Ackworth Moor Top, was appointed sole Commissioner by virtue of an Act of Parliament passed in 1817, entitled "An Act for inclosing lands in the Township of Trawden in the Chapelry of Colne in the Parish of Whalley in the County of Lancaster."

The Act recites that in the Forest of Trawden comprising the hamlets of Trawden, Winewall, and Wycollar, there were certain open and common pastures, moors, commons, commonable lands and waste grounds called by the names of Trawden Common, Winewall Common, Wycollar Common, and the Most Noble Elizabeth Duchess Dowager of Buccleuch and Queensbury was Lady of the said Manor of Colne and the Forest of Trawden, and as such was entitled to the soils of the said lands, and to all mines, minerals, and quarries of what nature or kind soever. Also the various copyhold tenants were entitled to certain rights of Common and Estover upon the above lands in proportion to the Copyhold rents then paid by them respectively. Also the said common lands were in their then state of little value and incapable of any considerable improvement, and that it would be of great advantage to the proprietors thereof and persons interested therein if the same were divided, allotted, and enclosed, but this could not be effected without the aid and authority of Parliament.

By the Enclosure Act, passed in 1801, these common lands in the Forest of Trawden should be valued, divided, and allotted as soon as conveniently might be. The Commissioner had to enquire concerning and if necessary fix the boundaries of the Forest. He had also power to set out and appoint public carriage roads and highways, and divert, turn, and stop up any of the roads upon any of the said lands. He had power to sell such lands on the extreme boundary as would raise money to defray all costs, charges, and expenses incident to the Act, award, copies, surveying, valuing, fencing and allotting, and all charges of the Commissioner, his assistants and necessary expenses. Proprietors who preferred to pay their share of the charges in money instead of sustaining a loss in land were at liberty to do so. The residue of the common land he allotted to the several owners and proprietors of ancient copyhold in proportion to the rents due from them to the Lord or Lady of the Manor.

The boundaries of the Forest are then accurately stated, beginning at Emmott Moor, across Boulsworth, to Will Moor Hill Nook. The roads set out include one public carriage road highway, 30 feet wide, beginning at the Haworth Turnpike Road near Comb Hill Cross, southwest through Smithy Scarrs, west to Wycollar Road at the east corner of Parson Lee Out Laithe, then to Turn Hole Clough south and southwest opposite Turn Hole Scarrs, west along the south side of the Flake to Beaver Nook, Beaver Cote, Lumb Laithe, Boulsworth Dyke, Gilford Scarrs, Will Moor Hill Flat, ending at the Township of Marsden near to Will Moor Hill Nook. The private roads are named as Antley, Will Moor Hill Clough, Saucer Clough, Slack Head, Winewall Common, and Green Wham Road.

Allotments for stone quarries for road repairing were made in Antley Scarrs and Saucer Hill Clough for Trawden; at the East End of the Flake and the Green Wham for Winewall; at Law Hill Clough and Comb Hill Scarrs for Wycollar.

Robin Hood's Well and 22 perches of land on the Haworth Road were allotted as a public watering place for cattle.

The allotments of common land are described in detail in the award, two demands being made on the recipients, first that good and sufficient fences must be made, and second, that a certain copyhold rent must be paid. In Trawden, the trustees of John Parr got 339 acres, the trustees of Mary Foulds 162 acres, and John Swinglehurst 70 acres, while Robert Towneley Parker bought 285 acres, John Swinglehurst bought 198 acres, and there were eight other smaller allotments, a total acreage of 1,221.

In Winewall, there were allotments to the trustees of Henry Owen Cunliffe, of Mary Foulds, and of John Parr, to James Wilson, and to Robert Midgley, with two sales of land, a total acreage of 1,089.

In Wycollar the trustees of Henry Owen Cunliffe received 476 acres by allotment, and 297 acres by purchase.

The total acreage included in the award was 3,398 acres, yielding a copyhold rent of £491/5/-.

To show how few people were eligible to share this common land, it may be of interest to state that in the Trawden portion only there were 13 allotments, while the population of Trawden Forest in that year was 2,507 persons, living in 470 houses.

The Award was signed at the Angel Inn, in Colne, in March, 1821, and as Trawden was then in Whalley Parish, the execution was proclaimed in the Parish Church of Whalley on the 1st April, 1821.

CHAPTER IV.

CORN GROWING AND THE OLD CORN MILL.

Until the middle of the last century there is little doubt that a considerable part of Trawden Forest was arable land. The only variety of corn grown was oats, and the ripening of this cereal, although `` is one that requires the least sunshine, was a source of much anxiety each year. Often the summer and autumn were so wet that the grain was spoiled, or was immature, when reaped, and when ground at the village corn mill it yielded an oatmeal which was frequently sharp and rather bitter to the taste. Oatmeal porridge, however, was the staple food.

Moses Hartley, now living, says that his father, at Dean House, always grew sufficient corn each year, and had it ground at the Trawden Mill until Laneshaw Bridge Mill was built.

Henry Driver, of Trawden, says that at Lodge Hill Farm they grew corn sufficient to provide an " oak kist " full of oatmeal, from which they made oatmeal porridge for every morning and evening meal throughout the year. The potatoes grown on the farm, and the pig, fattened every summer and killed, " in the back end of the year," furnished the regular mid-day meal of bacon and potatoes. Fresh butchers' meat they scarcely saw from one year end to another. From this it is obvious that the farmers then were self-supporting almost, and on this monotonous diet were reared men of fine physique, who lived to a good old age.

Thomas Chadwick's great-grandfather, known as " Old Jack Bannister," lived to the age of 84 years. He used to cut the corn for " Old John " Bannister, of Nichol House, and he also went every year for sixty years harvesting in the Doncaster district. His best earnings were two shillings per day.

There is no record of harvest rejoicings when the last load had been safely gathered in, but there was a custom for the children to have a portion of the first meal ground at the corn mill, to mix it with treacle, and have a feast of the sweetmeat, called, " traycle-dough," the last word having a guttural sound.

A poet tells about his father cutting the corn in or near Hollin Hall about 1850, but the last places where corn was regularly grown were at Alderbarrow, and on the slopes of the hill leading from Carry Bridge to the Mirage.

The corn mill stood on the site of the present Rock Hotel, and there are still traces of the mill dam, and the water channels leading to and from it. Previous to its erection, in 1566, the tenants took their corn to be ground at the Colne Corn Mill. In 1513, they covenanted with John Holgate, Robert Walcar, and John Hegyn to repair the road to the King's Mill in Colne before the feast of the Invention of the Holy Cross next ensuing, under pain of forfeiting 3s. 4d. In 1551, there was a complaint against James Bawden, of the King's Mill, at Colne, for taking excessive toll of his neighbours' meal.

At the Halmot Court, in 1566, by virtue of a Commission, Queen Elizabeth granted certain lands in Trawden, at the special request of Henry Farrer, and directed her trusty and well-beloved John Towneley, Esq., Steward of Blackburnshire, as follows : " Whereas it appeareth by the Certificate made by force of a Commission in November last concerning a survey and inquiry to find in what place within the Forest of Trawden a water corne mylne should be most fit, meet, and convenient to be builded, as well for the better course of the water as also for the ease of all our tenants, there is no place within the said forest, meeter, apter, or more convenient to build and erect the said mill upon, than upon a piece of copyhold ground called Blackscarr Croft, and that the owners by copyhold of the said parcel of ground are willing and consenting thereto, as well for the ease and commodity of themselves as for all other of our tenants thereabouts ; and that the water raise for the dam of the said mill must be taken up at a place called Graneforth Hole, being distant from the said ground forty roods. And that the tenant of the said mill being bounden to the building and repairing thereof at his own charges in all things, the mill will be worth yearly to us, above all the charges to be letten, five shillings, as by the same certificate remaining of record in our Duchy Chamber at Westminster now plainly appeareth.

And for as much as our well beloved Henry Farrer hath borne all charges of commission and execution, We therefore are contented and pleased that he and his heirs shall have, hold, and enjoy at will by copy of court roll the parcel of ground called Blackscarr Crofte and mill to be builded with all the soke, suit, easement and profit which may to the same belong, paying yearly to us, our heirs and successors, a yearly rent of five shillings, and doing such customs, suits and services as other Copyholders of our said Manor do or ought to do.

Therefore we charge you at the next Court to receive the surrenders of the copyholders of the premises whereupon the said mill shall be builded into our hands to the use of Henry Farrer and his heirs. Also cause to be entered on record in the Court Rolls there, the parcel of ground, the water course to the mill, the soke and suit of the tenants to the mill, to the said Henry Farrer and his heirs. Further grant lease that it should be lawful for him to erect, build and new make up at his own costs and charges, one Water Corn Mill, to have the course of water to the same together with the soke and suit. Thereupon admit him tenant to the mill, paying yearly five shillings and also such fine for his admittance as he ought to do. And hereof fail you not as you tender our pleasure. Given at our Palace of Westminster, the 21st day of July in the 7th year of our Reign."

By virtue of this Commission, James Foldes surrendered into the Queen's hands a parcel of land lying in Beardshawbooth of the yearly rent of one penny, containing half an acre of land, for the erection of a water corn mill and dam and stream, to the use of Henry Farrer, who was admitted tenant of the mill and its appurtenances on payment of a fine of five shillings.

In the next year, however, this gentleman sold his rights to James Hargreaves, of Lower Barrowford, and Lawrence Robinson, of Over Barrowford. A new and important condition seems to have been introduced at this transaction. "In consideration and recompence of the costs and charges which the copyholders have made and sustained touching and in the erection of the said mill, it shall be rated proportion like with the rest of the forest. Also four honest and discreet persons shall be elected and chosen by the copyholders from time to time for evermore to be supervisors of the mill, dam, race of water, wears, ways and all other commodities, and to judge, limit, and award, after what manner and within what time and space, reparations should be made of such premises, which shall be in ruin or decay, if any such happen, and in whom the fault is. When any supervisor shall depart, then one other honest and discreet person shall in like

24

manner be elected in his place.   And this order of choosing and appointing supervisors for the laudable upholding of the said mill, and to the common weal of the owners or customary tenants to continue and to be used from time to time for ever.   Likewise, the choosing of the miller to serve the mill from time to time and for ever to pass in like manner and form.   Provided that if any tenant make default in doing his duty touching any manner of costs the interest and inheritance of that party shall from henceforth be vested in the residue of the customary tenants."

In a rental of James I.. in 1608, one item is, "one copyhold water corn milne belonging to all the copyholders, rent, 5s. 1d."   For the next two centuries the mill was carried on presumably in accordance with the original intent.   When repairs were necessary the copyholders would be called on.

In an account book of Miss Mary Foulds, of Trawden Hall, in 1789, there are recorded assessments for the Trawden Mill, and a payment for grinding wheat there; also a refund of cash advanced in the previous year.

In 1836, James Pilling Foulds, of Trawden Hall, records in his diary, which is in the possession of W. Arthur Pilling, Esq., that he attended a meeting of the Trawden Mill Masters at the Rock Inn to ascertain if they had the power of letting the corn mill for other purposes than grinding corn.   From a Colne lawyer's (Mr. Bolton) written opinion, it was thought not, but he was directed to search the Court Rolls for other writings and reports.   In 1840, he also recorded that Mr. Midgley and himself met at the Rock Inn respecting the present tenant at Trawden Mill, who was not giving satisfaction, but as no other Mill Master attended, they did not do anything.   In 1845 he bought meal and Indian wheat from Henry Hartley, of the Trawden Mill.

The mill was last rented and worked by my grandfather, John Bannister, who paid £10 yearly rent to Mr. Midgley, the last of the old Mill Masters.   When Mr. Midgley died, his heirs had no title to the mill, and as John Bannister had left it some time before, in 1857, it remained unused, and was gradually broken up and looted by the neighbours, until, in 1880, it was completely destroyed.   It was sold by the township to Messrs. Critchley and Co., who never used it, and from whom the present owners of the site, Messrs. W. and T. Chadwick, bought it.

The last miller used to receive for the corn, ground, 2s. per pack of 240 lbs. The water rights included the stream near Beaver Gate, which came from near the Blue Slate Moor, above Brink Ends Farm. Formerly there were frequent disputes between the miller and the tenants of Trawden and of Wycollar about this water supply.

There is a tradition of a former miller, who lived at Cowfield, who was known as the "Gert Miller," or " Big Joany," who was an exceptionally strong man. He could carry five packs of 240 lbs. each, at once; one in his teeth, two on his back, and one under each arm. He could stoop down and raise a pack from the ground over on to his back, and walk with it to his home, over a mile away, without resting on the way.

The last miller was always called " Young John," because his father was also named John, and therefore was better known as "Old John." His own eldest son was also a John, so he was distinguished even after he reached manhood as "Little John," or, even better, as " Little John o' Young John's o' Old John's." Such was the excellent method of distinguishing three successive holders of the same name.

CHATPER V.

THE COAL INDUSTRY.

The oldest local industry, next to that of agriculture, is that of coal getting. It has already been mentioned that sea coal was mined and sold in Trawden in 1296, and in 1304.

In 1531, Henry Emot was fined 4d. for breaking soil on the King's waste in Beardshaw, at a place called Catholeclogh, and there winning carbunculæ (small coals), without licence. In this year of grace, 1921, owing to the long coal strike and the great scarcity of coals, many Trawden people have won small coals, after much trouble and risk, at this place, which retains the name it had 500 years ago.

In the yearly account of the Master Forester for 1422, he records the receipt of 13s. 4d. from coal mines, demised to Edmund Parker, in Troudene, and in 1434 the rent of coal mines in Colne and Troveden was 30s.

In 1662, the Duke of Albemarle instructed his steward to enquire after any coal mines that have been illegally digged in Trawden, and in the Inquisition next following the jury declare that formerly " there hath been a coal mine in Trawden and coal gotten therein, and that by Anthony Freiston and John Hobart, gentlemen, who had the same mine by force and virtue of a lease thereof to them made by King Charles the First, for and during the term, time, and space of thirty and one years from the feast of St. Michael the Archangel, 1639, and they have paid all the reversion and remainder of the said term, but no coals are now gotten there."

One of the most interesting local documents relating to this industry has been preserved among the Foulds' M.S., from Trawden Hall, by Mr. W. A. Pilling. The handwriting is very neat, but extremely difficult to decipher, owing to the change in the character of the letters since that time. Internal evidence assigns it to about the year 1621. It is a Bill of Complaint from James Folds against Margaret Hartley, concerning the taking of a coal mine at Lee, in the township of Marsden, and begins thus :—" In all humbleness complaining, unto your good Lordship, your poor and daily Orator, James Folds, of Lee, in the township of Marsden, in the County of Lancaster, husbandman. That whereas your said Orator and one

Margaret Hartley on or about Michaelmas Day had speeches and meetings for and about the taking and letting of one coal mine belonging to the said Margaret Hartley, and that your Orator should have the coal mine, and there were articles of agreement drawn between them, and they became bound either to other in the sum of £40 apiece, with conditions as follows :—First, it was fully agreed between the said parties that your Orator, his heirs, and assigns, should have, occupy, and enjoy the coal mine, for one whole year next ensuing after the feast day of St. Michael the Archangel then last past and pay at the end of every quarter £6 10s. od. of lawful money of England, and if the coal mine did wear out or decay before the end of the year, that then your Orator should but pay rateably for as long as he did get coals in the said mine. Lastly, that he should fill up the pit which he sinked and should but get coals at one shaft at a time. For one quarter your Orator well and truly paid the sum of £6 10s. od., and as the mine was then in decay, yielded up the mine to her satisfaction.

She promised to deliver an acquittance and the said bond to be cancelled, but in fair and flattering words she deferred to deliver the bond, always alleging that it was amongst divers other writings, but as soon as she could find it she would deliver it.

Now your Orator, knowing her to be a very covetous and hard-dealing woman, in September last demanded the bond again of the said Margaret Hartley at a fair held at Gisburn, near to her dwelling, and told her that if she would not keep her promise he would take some course to call it from her, whereupon the said Margaret Hartley then said there was some part of the rent unpaid and unless he would give her 20 nobles she would take the whole forfeiture of the £40 against him and contrary to all honesty, equity, justice, right, and good conscience, commenced a suit at common law against your Orator to his great loss, damage and good name. This unconscionable dealing is likely to tend to the utter overthrow and impoverishment of your Orator, his wife and children. May it therefore please your good Lordship to grant His Majesty's most Gracious Writ to be delivered to the said Margaret Hartley commanding her to stay and surcease the said suit and at a certain day and under a certain pain to appear before your Lordship in the Court of Chancery to answer to the premises and to abide by such order as your Lordship shall be thought to stand with equity, right, and good conscience, and your said Orator as nevertheless in all duty bound shall ever pray for your Lordship's health and prosperity in all happiness long to continue."

The last coal mining in Trawden was at the Lark Hill Colliery, which was opened up about 1874, as a continuation of the Fox Clough Colliery, through which the water drained. Ellis Blackburn was the manager, and his sons, John and Ellis Blackburn, have kindly supplied me with information and maps.

The coal was removed until they came to some old workings in the Cathole Clough, when they were flooded out. In these old workings several tools were discovered of a very antiquated type, showing that the coal had been won from there at a far distant date. The scoop, shaft, and handle of a shovel were made entirely of wood, no iron being used at all. There were baskets in which the coal had been carried and other entirely wooden implements. They were not surface workings, some shafts being 40 feet deep. The locality was near the footbridge that crosses the beck in Cathole Clough.

Its proximity to Beardshaw Farm on the opposite side of the valley led me to connect it with the earliest settlers in Trawden, thirty years before the actual references to these early coal mines were found.

Several shafts near Carry Heys and "The Old Engine" were worked at an earlier date than those of Fox Clough and Lark Hill.

In 1880 the price of coal from the Trawden pit was fourpence per cwt.

CHAPTER VI.

THE COTTON WEAVING INDUSTRY.

During the first half of the nineteenth century, Trawden, like many other East Lancashire villages, was a centre for hand-loom weaving. The last hand-loom weavers in the village were "Lad Walton," in the Upper Town, and "Bill Toit" (William Tillotson), in Church Street, or Smithy Lane as it was then called. Hand-loom weavers earned from seven to eight shillings per week, living almost entirely on porridge with skimmed or "old" milk, and were glad to get sufficient of this monotonous diet.

David Pickles, butter factor, related in my hearing in 1890, how he in his younger days earned 10½d. per day, and for food had no change from the above diet.

"Forester," Barnard Hartley, told me that as a young man he earned one shilling for a long hard day's work.

Some cottagers had their own hand-looms, and carried the yarns and woven cloth to and fro in large "hardin" bags called "piece poorks." The small manufacturers were called "putters out," and their houses or shops were often called "dandy shops," where hand-looms were let out to weavers who were too poor to own a hand-loom. Sometimes a weaver would retain some weft or warp and sell it to a shady broker. This illicit trading was called "rawnging," and is said to have been very prevalent and to have led to the failure of some manufacturers, e.g., Wm. Pilling, of Dogbottom, in 1850. On the other hand, many people were credited with having obtained either goods or money by this fraudulent practice. The putters out often kept a grocer's shop, and did a "truck shop" business, i.e., gave a note of credit on the employer's shop for goods up to a certain value, instead of wages.

Once a Scotch merchant persuaded Old John o' Absaloms, Henry o' Aarons, and John Whalley, all putters out, that he could give them much better prices than they were receiving, obtained all their cloth, and then failed or disappeared. This ruined all the local putters out, and this extensive collapse completed the gradual decay of this home industry, which was being supplanted by the advent of the power-loom.

Hand-loom weaving was most irksome to the young men, who had perforce to remain indoors the livelong day, bending over the loom and sending the shuttle from side to side, but when the evening brought them release it is not surprising to learn that they were ready for any kind of adventure or practical joking that a leader could suggest. The call of the moors also could not be resisted.

There was no age limit for children to begin working. As soon as a child could learn she had to wind bobbins of weft for the weaver. For bobbin winding at home the rate of pay was 2/6 per bundle, but after the first winding machine was erected at the Lane House Mill, for exactly the same work only 1/6 was paid. Similar reductions occurred in cotton weaving, so that the home industry could not live side by side with the factory system.

THE COTTON FACTORIES.

Pave Mill or "Salts," was built by William Marsden, who bought Trawden Hall and lived there. The older part was formerly a "dandy" house. A coal gas installation was set up for the use of this mill, and gas was supplied to Scar Top Mill for 14/- per thousand cubic feet. Even at this price it was a great improvement on the preceding system of having a tallow candle or a paraffin oil lamp over each loom. Erasmus Marsden, son of William Marsden, has now a very old and interesting birth certificate relating to "Robert Filius Henrici Marsden de Gisborne, generosi, 1683." (Robert the son of Henry Marsden, of Gisburn, gentleman), which shows their importance long ago.

Brooks Shed or "Dogbottom" was built by "Little Will," William Pilling, about 1860, and extended by Messrs. W. and T. Chadwick later. Many manufacturers have commenced business there and then removed to larger premises. It was first occupied by John and James Pilling before they removed to Colne.

"Scar Top Mill," or "Shipley," was built by my grandfather, John Bannister, while he was the corn miller, and rented by James Preston, who afterwards removed to Walk Mill, Colne. John Bannister and Sons then occupied it. The "New End" of this mill, an enlargement, was built entirely of material from Wycollar Hall, which was then being dismantled and sold piece-meal. At the same time he bought and removed the "haunted chamber" and the front doorway and entrance hall, and erected them behind his own house, where they still remain unchanged. This haunted chamber used to be the play-room and workshop for my brothers and myself, and from personal experiences extending over many dark evenings I can swear that the ghost did not migrate with the building. The outer gate pillars were also removed and placed in Church Street at the entrance to the mill road. They were massive square columns composed of hewn rectangular blocks surmounted by pyramidal capitals, and stood about nine feet high. These structures were originally almost exactly opposite the end of the stone foot bridge by which Wycollar Hall ruins are approached.

About 1890 this mill was bought by a Mr. Brindle, who started a chemical factory for making guncotton from cotton waste, but this industry had only a short life. It is now partly a weaving shed and partly a laundry.

Lane House Mill, or Randolph's Mill, is the oldest mill in Trawden. The earliest power-loom manufacturer was named William Wilkinson. About 1840 it was owned and run by John Smith, from whose son Randolph it received its name. There were two other sons, Joshua and Fred, and another mill, that of Lodge Holme, was in charge of Joshua. At a later date Mr. Joshua Smith removed to Colne, then to Burnley in 1878.

Mr. Joshua Smith had two sons, Cicero and Fred, who developed their father's business by building a shed at Cornholme for 2,000 looms, and extending the Manchester side of the firm's activities. Both Cicero Smith, Esq., now of Southport, and Lord Colwyn, of Colwyn Bay, who was formerly Sir Fred Smith, have won great renown not only for business ability and successes, but because they have been earnest religious and social workers, being particularly interested in temperance work and in the Y.M.C.A.

A daughter of John Smith married John Pilling, the father of Randolph S. Pilling, architect, of Colne.

Another daughter married Robert Chapman, who was in the Charge of the Light Brigade in the Crimean War, and afterwards fought in the Indian Mutiny. In the Public Library of Colne there is a letter from this man describing the rounding up and pursuit of the rebel soldiers.

Lane House Mill had been a three-storied "dandy shop" before power looms were introduced, and the first engine there had a boiler with no safety valve fitted to it. Across the road in later days there was a gas yard where coal gas was made, and Alderman R. Foulds, of Colne, once told me that this installation was of earlier date than any other in Trawden or in Colne.

Adjoining this mill was "Pilling's Shop," in which began the business of John Pilling, loom makers, of Colne. This family of Pilling was not connected with the Pillings of Trawden Hall, but owned Alderhurst End Farm, then called "Pilling's Farm." John Pilling was a joiner, who made hand-looms, and then commenced making improved looms during the transition period when power-looms were displacing hand-looms. He had no foundry, so the castings were obtained at Clitheroe and carted to Trawden, to make looms of a type intermediate in character between the old wooden hand-loom and the modern power-loom with considerably more wood in them than the modern power-loom has. At that date he must have been alert for new ideas, because in 1848, James Pilling Foulds, of Trawden Hall, recorded in his diary that he had spent one evening from 7 to 11 o'clock with John Pilling, joiner, of Lane House, "engaged with Coulson's Slide Rule and Treatise which had cost 6/9, but we were not able either of us to understand it properly. John took the treatise with him."

Hollin Hall Mill was built and enlarged about 1850-1860. For a long period it was run by John and Steven Sagar.

Lodge Holme Mill derived its power from a water wheel fed by the water from a large mill dam in front of it. For many years it was empty, then it became a dye works, and now, after extensive enlargement, it is the home of the Multi-Colour Dyers.

Critchley's Mill, the Cotton Tree Mill, was built in 1847. A little later, an overlooker at this mill, named Tom o' Bobs, earned an unenviable notoriety for his smooth words in criticising cloth which was invariably followed by heavy "baiting," i.e., fining the weaver for flaws in the cloth.

The largest mill in Trawden, the Black Carr Mill, was commenced by a Committee of the inhabitants elected at a public meeting with the village schoolmaster, Mr. George Sowerby, in the chair, in February, 1880. The village was canvassed and subscriptions received sufficient to float a Limited Liability Mill Company. It was completed in 1882, and let off as room and power. Three years later it was extended to double its original size.

The Forest Shed was built about 1890.

The story that once there were windmills at Winewall and Windy Arbour is obviously absurd when one considers the abundant water power available in the district.

The most tragic period in a survey of this industry was during the great Cotton Famine of 1860-1870, when the supply of raw cotton from America was cut off, because of the war between the Northern and the Southern States. There are people living now who remember the extreme poverty and general starvation to which so many of the people were reduced. One lady can tell me of her mother reduced to the extreme limit, with no morsel of food and no coin in the house, yet so proud of her independence that when a curious neighbour entered the house unbidden at dinner time, the large "posnet" full of water only was warming on the fire to suggest that the end of her resources was not yet at hand. She built her hopes that day on her husband who had gone to his relations in Lothersdale for anything eatable. When he appeared in the afternoon at the top of "Dick Field," with a full sack and waved his handkerchief, it was a welcome signal.

At Oaken Bank, or "The Hole," a man lived named James Hartley, with a large family of children, who was brought to a much greater extremity. It was winter time with snow covering the ground. For two days he had had practically no food, giving the remains to his children, but one night the children had been put to bed crying for hunger. He was a Wesleyan class leader and local preacher, and that night he had to meet his class at Pilling's Farm. His wife thought that he was so weak with hunger that he would perish if he crossed the snow covered fields, and begged him to stay at home. He was a man of great faith, and still hoped that food would come, but in any case he would not miss his class meeting. On the way he felt something fluttering at his feet. It was pitch dark, but when he put his hands down he caught two large birds, and felt that there were others. Returning home he roused his oldest boys and returned for more of the game. They were wild geese or other large wild birds such as had never been seen in the district before. Some were taken to the village and sold and with the money obtained meal and milk were bought, so that the whole family could be fed with as much porridge as they desired when they had been roused from sleep.

James Hartley lived to a good old age, and always enjoyed narrating these facts, adding his certain conviction that God had tried his faith, and then sent these birds in abundance as a special reward at the moment of his utmost need, because he never looked back again, but prospered. To him it was always a striking instance of God's Providence.

From many sources "doles" were given to help extreme cases, and shopkeepers gave long credits, but for many long years there were some who remembered and told of their experiences with a look almost of horror. It emphasised the natural inclination to be thrifty and save all the money possible against the time of need that might come again. It may perhaps explain the fact that nearly every family in Trawden owns the house they live in, and has in addition a "good bit o' brass" put away in some Bank or Building Society or Limited Company.

CHAPTER VII.

THE RELIGIOUS DENOMINATIONS.

From the foundation of the parish of Colne, Trawden Forest was a part of this chapelry, and many entries of Trawden people occur in the earliest registers of baptisms, marriages, and deaths, which began in 1599.

The oldest sign of a religious community in Trawden is still engraved on a stone forming part of the Quaker Burial Ground on the Mirage. The inscription is "I.S. 1688," and for thirty years it remained copied in my notebook, waiting for explanation, until I had the good fortune to meet the one representative who could enlighten me on this point. To Mr. Thomas Foulds, of Stanley Villa, Colne, I am greatly indebted for information and assistance in recovering many old records.

THE QUAKERS.

The Quakers or Friends were the first religious body with a home in Trawden. The inscription above marks the initials of Jeffrey Shackleton, who by a deed poll dated 28th June, 1687, declared that he held a plot of land, which had been surrendered to him and others upon trust for a burial ground for Quakers. An additional plot was surrendered later to Roger Hartley and others, and in 1697 the first plot was said to have a meeting house erected thereupon, and on the second the trustees were to erect a stable. The meeting house, stable, and cottage were sold in 1850, and only the burial ground now remains. In secluded spots such as Trawden Forest the Quakers were strong in numbers in those days of bitter persecution, and because of their seclusion they were able to retain the simple ways and beliefs of the earlier Friends for a considerable time. Moreover change would be long in coming to such an agricultural community, so there would not be the constant temptation to fall away from the distinctive customs as would occur in the towns. In 1652 the founder of this body, George Fox, paid a visit to Pendle Hill, where he had a vision of his future work, but he does not appear to have come into this immediate neighbourhood.

Records of business meetings were carefully kept, and we had the good fortune to discover their present resting place. The Trawden meeting was an offshoot from that of Marsden, and the first notice of Trawden occurs in 1688, when Roger Hartley and Ellen Hartley give notice of marriage. Until 1734 there were joint business meetings for

Marsden and Trawden, then from 1734 to 1821 Trawden held separate meetings. Owing to the diminishing numbers in Trawden, the union of the Trawden and Marsden Meetings took place in 1821, and continued until 1844, when the name of Trawden disappears from the minute book of the Marsden Meeting. For some years previous to this date the Trawden Friends had met at Park House, Colne, the residence of John and Mary Hall.

Names of the members of these meetings show that many households included or consisted of Quakers. The most important family, however, were the Wilsons, the descendants of Thomas Wilson, who settled at Beaver Farm in 1710. He had taken his full share of the "discipline" of the Society in Keighley in 1700, having been despoiled of his goods for non-payment of tithes, and this may account for his desire for the seclusion of Trawden Forest. His descendants are numerous, and the family history was compiled a few years ago by one of them, Wilfred Wilson, solicitor, of Manchester.

The eldest son of Thomas Wilson was Richard, nicknamed "Silvershins," a serge weaver and yeoman farmer. The third son, Thomas, lived at Gilford Clough, and then at Meadow Bottoms, which has probably been owned by Wilsons ever since. The fifth son was a schoolmaster, and the wife of the sixth son, Ann Wilson, who lived in Wycollar Dene, and died in 1753, is described as having been a minister for 20 years. The last Quakers in Trawden were John and Jane Wilson, who built the present house at Meadow Bottoms. They had two sons, Thomas and John, who took no active part as Friends, and the last interment in the Burial Ground was of the above Thomas Wilson in 1881.

The simple quiet dress and the distinctive customs and beliefs of these early Quakers are now only traditions to many people, so that an authentic account of local records may not be out of place.

A Friend could only marry a member of the Society. If he married outside, "a woman of the world," by a priest, he was reported and disowned. This disciplinary measure was also applied if he was reported for disorderly walking out, or for having been "sprinkled." About 1850 the rigid rule concerning marriage within the Society was withdrawn. A typical marriage minute relating to Trawden Friends in 1693 is as follows:—"Joshua Fielding of Swinshead and Mary Veepond of Lane House, the second time laid their intentions of marriage with each other before this meeting, and inquiry having been made in the wonted manner they are found clear upon all accounts and we leave them to their liberty in Truth to accomplish their said intentions when they see meet. and this meeting appoints Stephen Sagar and Henry Veepond to see the accomplishment thereof and bring account with a copy of the certificate to the monthly meeting to be hereafter recorded.''

Women were treated as equal in every respect to men, but there were many rules regarding their dress. They were advised to keep down needless superfluities, and forbidden to dress the head high, or with a needless pinch in the middle of the forehead; or to have linen with double borders and pinched about; or to have hoods with long tabbs turned back any more at cheek than at brow; or necklaces or strings about their necks. They must have no black or white tippets plaited or welted about, no mantyres lined with black or other very different colours with long small tails pinned according to the fashion of the world, no stomachers that are faced with stuff or stripes of divers colours, no gowns with peaks behind and muslin aprons, no fashionable girdles pinned with borders, no painted calico in frocks or aprons, no children's linen with welts or needless work in them, and no hats with broad ribbons tied with a bunch behind.

At a Trawden business meeting in 1699, there is the minute, "Upon consideration of the odiousness of sleeping in Meetings this Meeting doth think requisite that two friends in each meeting, viz., Marsden and Trawden, be appointed to take care that such as are over-burdened with this infirmity be spoken to and exhorted to diligence and watchfulness against the same, pursuant to which this meeting doth appoint William Sagar and Edward Veepond for Marsden and James Bancroft and Francis Robinson for Trawden, that so the evil may be removed from God's camp and diligence may increase among them, and so the blessing of God will rest among them as on the Israel of God, even the dew of Hermon and the fatness of enduring blessedness.''

Friends were advised to stand clear of the customs of this world as in the giving or receiving gloves, ribands, scarves, or any such like things at marriages or burials, not to use any coverings upon their coffins, nor colour them any colour, nor make great provision at funerals.

Smoking was frequently discountenanced as being "inconsistent with our holy profession and such as have occasion to use it should take it privately, neither in their labour or employment, nor by the highways, nor in the alehouses, nor elsewhere in public."

They should stand clear of making, wearing, or selling any striped, flowered, or figured cloth, stuff, or silk, and be careful in their apparel to avoid over wide skirted coats and great long cuffs, cross pockets, side sleeves overful, skirted coats and broad hems on cravats.

They were frequently reminded to take care to settle their estates by will and otherwise whilst in health to prevent future trouble, must not attend fairs and such like meetings, must seek permission to visit other parts of the country, must not overcharge themselves in trade, and must stand clear of making any provision for the observation of that time commonly called Christmas. Friends must not resist against outward governments nor enter into controversies on this world's kingdoms; they must not pay church tithes, or steeple house levies as they were termed, and they must be careful to live within their incomes.

Often they were persecuted, and their sufferings were recorded. In 1653 William Dewsbury, being moved to go to Colne, he declared the word of God to the people at the market cross, until he was pulled down by one James Foster and hurried along the street to the end of the town. In 1662 at a meeting which was held at the house of James Hartley, in Trawden, the officers entered and finding John Moor upon his knees engaged in prayer, they violently plucked him away and haled him before John Starkey, the Justice so called, who committed him a prisoner to Lancaster Castle, where he remained upwards of eleven weeks. At the same time, John Hartley, Peter Shackleton, James Hartley, and Samuel Driver were apprehended, and upon their refusal to take the **oath** which was tended by the said John Starkey, they were also **imprisoned** for eleven weeks, and the constable took a horse worth four marks and two sheep worth 12/- for the taking of them to prison.

In 1695 Roger Hartley was released after an imprisonment of over four years, but in the next following year for threepence demand, and sixpence charges, he had taken from him three pewter dishes and three iron chains, and a plough tackle worth 17/-.

The strict observance of the many rules of conduct, and the compulsory wearing of the Quaker dress, would naturally lead to a decline in membership, but still more serious was the loss of the missionary

39

spirit of the founders, which led both men and women ministers to spare no effort and endure any suffering in spreading abroad the Truth, as they believed it. Certain it is, that many of their principles are being accepted by the world to-day, although this denomination is now so few in numbers.

Of these solemn and earnest seekers after Truth, whose profession was accompanied by self-denial and suffering, no representative now remains in Trawden, and no memorial marks their past existence save the little grass covered burial ground on the Mirage.

THE INGHAMITES.

The religious denomination next in order is that of the Inghamites, who built a Meeting House at Winewall in 1752. The founder of this body was Mr. Benjamin Ingham, a native of Osset, Dewsbury, in Yorkshire. He was born in 1712, received a liberal education at Batley School, and Queen's College, Oxford, which he entered in 1730. During his residence in Oxford he became acquainted with Charles Wesley, John Wesley, and other devout and earnest students, who afterwards became great public characters. In 1735 he was ordained to the ministry by the Bishop of Oxford. On the same day he commenced preaching, and preached his first sermon to the prisoners in Oxford Castle. In consequence of a pressing invitation for his assistance in preaching from Mr. John Wesley, he sailed to Georgia, remained there for a year and some months, and visited Carolina and Pennsylvania before he returned to England. Returning to his native place, Ossett, he renewed his labours as a preacher in the Established Church, preaching in all the churches and chapels in the neighbourhood, with such success that great numbers of people attended wherever he proclaimed his message. This roused the jealousy of the clergy, and they prohibited him their churches and chapels, on which he commenced to preach in the fields, barns, and houses, while his converts continued to increase in number. These were formed into Societies, nearly sixty in Yorkshire, which were visited once a month by Mr. Ingham or those who assisted him.

In 1743 Mr. Ingham first commenced preaching in Lancashire, at Colne Edge, near Colne, in consequence of a solicitation of some of the residents there. Two years later, while Mr. Ingham was in Germany, Mr. W. Batty was the principal preacher. At this time Mr.

Wesley's preachers appeared in Craven and Lancashire, and John Wesley himself came to Roughlee, where Mr. Batty was also labouring. They had much conversation upon religion, and Mr. Wesley tried, but without success, to persuade Mr. Batty to connect himself with his party. Mr. Ingham soon returned from Germany, and continued his labours with increasing success. Labourers and converts were frequently abused and mobbed with such violence that often their lives were in danger, but this did not abate their zeal. Societies were formed, a Steward appointed over them, and they were visited by itinerant preachers or Elders once a week or once a fortnight. At one of their general meetings, held at Winewall, in 1753, Mr. Ingham gave a long letter of advice to all his fellow preachers. Most of their Meeting Houses were built between 1750 and 1757. Mr. Ingham intended to form the societies into some regular order with Elders and teachers over each, but found so great a difficulty in obtaining qualified persons that he decided to continue the itinerant plan a little longer.

In 1762 Mr. Ingham was chosen to be Elder at Tadcaster, where he laboured until his death in 1772. In 1741 he had married the Right Honourable Lady Margaret Hastings, sister to the Earl of Huntingdon. He was not only an earnest preacher, but was very liberal in relieving the needy, and in his later years he wrote a treatise on the faith and hope of the gospel.

In 1762 there were twenty to thirty church members at Winewall. They chose John Slinger, Elder, and Robert Waddington and James Walker, Deacons. William Edmondson was chosen Elder in 1780, and the next Elders were James Bellhouse and Henry Bannister.

Among the trustees of the first Winewall Chapel two were described as shalloon weavers, and one, as a calimanco weaver. The present chapel was built in 1860, and the old chapel, enlarged, became a Sunday and day school. Mr. C. Gibbon, of Colne, was the first trained certificated schoolmaster, and he was followed by Mr. R. Sowerbutts, who retained this post until the school was closed.

In 1814 there were thirteen Inghamite Churches in England, the largest being at Wheatley, with 56 members, while Winewall was the next with 41 members. These churches had then united with The Scots Old Independent Churches, and a book of historical sketches, published by H. Earnshaw, printer, of Colne, in 1814, gives the history of the two bodies with the correspondence which led to their union.

At Brantford, in Canada, there is now an Inghamite Church, founded by emigrants from Winewall.

THE WESLEYAN METHODISTS.

In 1810 the Wesleyan Methodists, who had previously attended the Colne Lane Chapel, erected their chapel at the most convenient situation for the needs of the three hamlets. The site called the potato croft was part of an estate called Jumb, a name which is still retained in the Jumb Pit. The first trustees were Richard Sagar, of Southfield, merchant; Thomas Wilkinson, of Colne, grocer; Christopher Lister, of Colne, ironmonger; George Battinson, of Colne, tinner; William Hartley, grocer; Nathan Pickles, grocer; James Hartley, of Hoyle, cotton weaver; James Greenwood, of Lane House, weaver; Henry Hartley, of Upper Town, weaver; George Frankland, weaver; John Heaton, of Wellhead, weaver; and John Dean, of Southfield in Great Marsden, weaver. The chapel had to be held on trust for the people called Methodists, and used for preachers to expound the Scriptures according to the doctrines contained in the first four volumes of sermons and notes upon the New Testament as set forth by the Reverend John Wesley. Pew rents were to be received, and, after other charges were met, were to be applied towards the support of the itinerant Methodist preachers. In the original deed the vendor and one trustee make their marks in place of the usual signature. This deed is of interest as being of earlier date than 1832, the date of the "model deed," to which all deeds of later date in the Wesleyan Methodist Church are referred.

Tradition says that Miss Mary Foulds warmly sympathised with these people, and had offered to give them an excellent site in Whitely Carr, adjoining Church Street. The short-sighted opposition to this offer checked her generosity, and lost both a valuable site and support from a wealthy local patron.

The Sunday School, held in the body of the chapel, was mainly concerned with the teaching of reading, only the older members receiving didactic instruction. This was often the only schooling that members were able to obtain during their childhood and youth. A set of rules, published in 1816, gave very precise instructions for superintendents, teachers, and children, and an address to parents. The school hours were from 9 to 12 a.m. and 1-30 to 4-30 p.m., from Lady Day to Michaelmas, and for the rest of the year from 10-15 to 12 a.m. and 1-30 to 4 p.m. The superintendent had to open and close the school with singing and prayer, but not to employ more than ten minutes in this exercise, to supply books, organise the scholars, advise teachers, and maintain discipline. If children habitually came late or were absent without satisfactory reason, or misbehaved, they would be excluded from the school. In the address to parents they are respectfully informed that the design of this institution is "The welfare of the rising generation," and "all who take an active part in it, do it without fee or pecuniary reward, as men of God who labour to do all the good they can."

Class meetings of members were held in various cottages, a practice which has not yet died out.

The most important event of the year has always been the Sunday School Sermons, called the "Charity" or "Rushbearing." This was always a great musical festival, new music for hymns and anthems being sought for far and wide. Additional vocalists and all kinds of wind and stringed instruments were requisitioned. The lady members of the choir, dressed in white, sat on a stage built round the pulpit. On that day the seating accommodation was taxed to its limit, as members of other denominations, old residents, and friends, made a special effort to be there. In 1850 the chapel was enlarged, and in 1890 it was partly re-built and restored to its present form. Centenary services were held in 1910, and a booklet published, giving many details of the history of the place and people.

In 1903, the old-time "Charity" having been discontinued for some years, there was a revival of a phenomenal character, organised by the older members and friends. Mr. Thomas Shaw and Mr. Henry Pickles canvassed the old scholars, and found them equally enthusiastic in desiring an "Old Time Charity." Mr. Shaw erected a stage, and a former choirmaster, Mr. H. W. Bannister, trained old scholars, including grandmothers and great-grandmothers, to sing, not only the old hymns and anthems, but later anthems from the "Messiah," "Creation," and "12th Mass." The services were a great success, and were repeated on several occasions, the unique choir singing at no less than twenty services.

43

In the chapel vestry, on the side nearest the river, there was formerly a day school. Following the 1870 Education Act the present Sunday school was erected and opened as a Wesleyan Day School in 1873. Mr. J. G. Tolton was the first headmaster. He was succeeded by Mr. G. Sowerby, who resigned in 1887, and was followed by Mr. A. Wilmore, now D.Sc. of London University, who remained in charge until 1896. Mr. T. Little then took charge, and continued until the present Council School was erected, to which he and the children were then transferred.

The first member of the Trawden Society to enter the ranks of the ministry was the Rev. James Walton, who volunteered for service as a Wesleyan Methodist Missionary in Sierra Leone, West Africa, after his three years' training in Richmond Wesleyan College, in 1902. After a long service there he has returned home to circuit work.

In 1906 he married Miss M. J. Bannister, of Trawden, who had just completed her training as a nurse at the London Hospital. They reached Freetown early in October, and during the next month made a long missionary tour through the hinterland, reaching many places where no white woman had previously been seen. On the return journey she had an attack of malarial fever, was prostrated for several weeks, and then invalided home as a last hope. She died at Trawden, five days after reaching England, on February 22, 1907, one of the many missionary men and women whom the West African Field has claimed.

THE PRIMITIVE METHODISTS.

The first foreign missionary from Trawden was a Primitive Methodist named William Hartley, who went to Australia during the first great rush to the gold diggings. On one occasion during his travels he announced to a company of gold diggers that he was going to preach that evening in their camp, and gave them an invitation to attend. There was an immediate response by one of the diggers named John o' Anns (John Bracewell), who claimed recognition as an old Trawden acquaintance.

This denomination began their services in Trawden in a room under the corner shop in Chapel Street. About 1826 they built a chapel, and had a burial ground attached, on the present site of Pave

Mill. In some way this chapel must have become the property of a very eccentric character, Edward James Taylor, who had once been a Primitive Methodist minister, because in 1850 he sold it for nineteen guineas to the following trustees :—John Hopkinson, weaver; David Pickles, butter factor; William Tattersall, weaver; James Pickles, weaver; and Mark Petty, of Coal Pit Lane, Colne, farmer. The trust declares that the premises are to be used in conformity with a deed poll under the hands and seal of Hugh Bourne, James Bourne, and William Clowes, dated 5th February, 1830, which relates to the doctrines and discipline of the society, and permits the building to be used as a day and Sunday school room, and also as a lecture room for the advocacy of the principles of total abstinence from intoxicating drinks, and for lectures on literary and scientific subjects, so as such lectures and school do not interfere with the religious services of the society. If any more eligible site for a chapel can be obtained within the hamlet of Trawden, they shall be at liberty to sell the premises and lay out the moneys. Any surplus money shall be applied in the first place in discharge of the debts owing on the Primitive Methodist Chapel at Laneshaw Bridge, near Colne, and in the next place on the discharge of the debts owing upon all the incumbered chapels of the Society within the Burnley Circuit.

A more suitable site for a larger chapel was found in 1875, when the present chapel was built.

The Hartley Memorial Sunday School was so named in memory of Sir William Pickles Hartley, whose father was a Trawden tradesman, and who has always responded most generously to every appeal for the church of his fathers.

THE INDEPENDENT METHODISTS.

The members of the Independent Methodist Free Church held their first religious services about the middle of the last century in a cottage chapel near the Lane House Mill, but these were discontinued when most of the members removed to Colne and founded the Providence Chapel in Waterside, and the old Bethel Chapel at Primet Bridge.

At a later date, returning members, joined by seceders from the other religious communities in Trawden, began to hold services in the Literary Institute, and soon afterwards built their present place of worship in 1882.

THE CHURCH OF ENGLAND.

The parish of Trawden was formed out of the parish of Christ Church, which had been formed out of the parish of Colne, which was once a part of the large parish of Whalley. The first Church services were held at Dog Bottom Cottage. At that time there was no bridge over the river, the highway forded the river a little higher up the valley, and a footpath crossed the river where the present Brook Shed stands.

J. P. Foulds, Esq., of Trawden Hall, gave the land on which the Church School was built in 1840, and also the stone required, which was obtained from the old Rock Lane Delph. A few years later he made similar bequests for the church itself. On both occasions his brother, William Pilling, who afterwards succeeded him at Trawden Hall, had to sign away from this property, as the heir at law.

The School was opened in August, 1840, and was used for Church services, and also as a day school, providing accommodation for 200 children. The cost of erection was covered by grants from the National Society, the Committee of Council, and private subscriptions. It was united with the National Society in June, 1843, when the Rev. A. Hodgson was incumbent of Christ Church.

The Church was erected in 1845, the foundation stone being laid by J. P. Foulds, Esq., J.P., on the 18th April of that year. It was dedicated to St. Mary the Virgin, as a means of perpetuating the memory of Miss Mary Foulds.

The Sentence of Consecration by the Bishop of Chester is dated 13th July, 1846, and states that the Church was erected because the parish of Christ Church was of great extent and contained a large population. This parish was then in the Chester Diocese, and the Church Deeds are still at the Diocesan Registry at Chester, because the Diocese of Manchester was not founded until 1848, two years afterwards.

The first curate in Trawden was a Mr. Pryce, who died in 1840. The next curate was William Messenger, who resided at Far Wanlass, and afterwards became vicar at Habergham Eaves.

The first vicar was the Rev. Thomas Craven Humfrey, who resided at Carry Bridge until the vicarage was built in 1857. The land was bought from the trustees who were administering the Trawden Hall Estate during the later years of Mr. J. P. Foulds, and the foundation stone was laid in 1857.

Mr. Humfrey has written on a plan of the Church, "This church was erected in the year 1845, and contains accommodation for 500 persons. A grant of £300 in aid of its erection was made by the Incorporated Society for providing the enlargement, building, and repairing of churches and chapels on condition that the seats for 346 persons described on the annexed plan should be set apart and declared to be free and unappropriated for ever."

The Church Registers begin in 1846, and early entries of marriages show by the mark of the cross that many people could not write their names.

Mr. Humfrey spent £500 on the vicarage, and during his first year obtained a certificated teacher for the day school at a salary of £100 per year; but as he lost £30 on this transaction, and his living was worth only £150, he fell back to an uncertificated teacher, Mr. Thomas Shaw.

Mr. Humfrey died in 1875, and was succeeded in 1876 by the Rev. William Lancaster Taylor, M.A., who laboured diligently in this parish until 1887. He found that the church was very dilapidated, much of the woodwork suffering from dry rot, and he spared no effort to renovate and beautify his church, increase the value of the living, and develop the interest and love for the Church Services. He visited every farm throughout the parish, started mid-week services at Wycollar, purchased three acres of land behind the vicarage and churchyard, increased the value of the living by £50, and in 1881 obtained permission to reseat the Church, to move the organ from the west gallery to form a chancel, for a prayer desk to be made, a portion of choir benches and a new lectern to be provided, heating apparatus to be altered and improved, and the church to be lighted with gas.

His last public benefit to his parish was to erect the clock in the church tower in 1887, the Jubilee year of Queen Victoria. In that year he exchanged livings with the Rev. James Wilkie Baron, of Sadberge, and is now living in retirement at St. Annes-on-Sea.

One of his sons "fell asleep" at Trawden, and is buried in the churchyard, while his three other sons successively had brilliant school and University careers at Oxford, all rising to eminence as clergymen of the Church of England.

Succeeding vicars have been the Rev. J. W. Baron, M.A., until 1898; the Rev. J. P. Petty, M.A., from 1898 to 1907; and the Rev. H. P. Dempsey, M.A., since that date.

The connection between the Church of England and the followers of John Wesley must have lingered on. My own ancestors in Trawden from 1810 were Wesleyans, but every member up to and including my father was baptised at the Colne Parish Church.

THE NATIONAL SCHOOL.

As stated above, Mr. Humfrey tried to found a school on modern lines. Being unable to do so, he recalled a local man, Mr. Thomas Shaw, who held the post of schoolmaster until 1866. At that time he was one of the very few men in the village who discarded the dialect and "talked fine." He had no assistants or grants, and was supported by school fees of twopence per week each for those who came to learn knitting, crotchet work, sampling, and general needlework, which formed the basis of the regular instruction, but the fee was fourpence per week for those scholars who aspired to write in copybooks.

Following Mr. Shaw in 1866, a shoemaker, named Thomas Dixon, held the post for about ten years, combining this office with that of rate collector. He was succeeded by several lady head mistresses, until the school was finally handed over to the School Board as an infants' school.

About 1860 there was a school kept in "The Streets" by John Bannister, "Little Hundred," run on simple lines, but no attempt was made to teach feminine accomplishments.

Similar schools were kept in the Winewall hamlet by James Bellhouse, and by Mrs. Bullock. The methods were crude and inefficient, and materials for instruction were scanty, but no others were available. The most striking incident in the memory of those who passed through these schools was the "barring out" before a holiday. Mrs. Bullock, for instance, was carried in her chair out of the room, while the children

48

chanted, "Pardon, Missis, pardon, pardon for a pin, if ye doant let us hev halliday we'll nivver let ye in." Then the holiday was announced, the teacher was admitted, and the breaking-up time came with rejoicing. Mrs. Bullock's main occupation was to knit stockings for people, and she continued knitting all day long, taking her scholastic duties as incidental. When learning to read, the children had first to point at the letters with a feather, which was an essential instrument for each scholar, then to wait patiently until the teacher was ready to judge if they had learned that a, b, spelled ab. The next step was to use the "reedy ma deezy" book (reading made easy), while the final stage of excellence was reached when they could read in the Bible. She had also a long mangle upstairs, which she allowed the villagers to use on payment of one penny for each occasion.

In the rather superior school kept by James Bellhouse, at Well Head, in Winewall, one old scholar says that she learnt to write there, but the one and only copy set for writing was, "Commandments ten, God gave to men." She learnt to write this sentence beautifully, but she learnt to write no other words, so that she could not sign her own name when she had finished schooling.

CHAPTER VIII.
OBSOLETE CUSTOMS. AND BELIEFS.

Some interesting customs have lapsed even during the last fifty years.

When a young man first sought the companionship of a fair lady, it was considered the correct custom for the lady to repel her lover with spirit to find out whether he was really in earnest or not. When this testing period had been successfully passed, other young people noticed when they first walked out together, followed them and demanded that they should keep up the old custom and "pay the pitcher." In Winewall it was called, "paying the fooitings." Woe to the man if he only gave sixpence, because then he would be frequently reminded that that was the sum at which he valued the woman he hoped to marry. If he paid one shilling or more, the word would be passed round that he had paid the pitcher, and the two young people in future would be free to go unmolested on their happy way.

Eighty years ago the happy pair who wished to enter the bonds of matrimony engaged a fiddler to march in front of them making joyous melody as they marched from the home of the bride to the church gates. When the ceremony had been completed, he again played his instrument in front of the wedding party, as they walked to the public house, where a dinner had been provided. "Old Jock" was one of the last fiddlers of this kind.

Even till very recent times the wedding party was obstructed by men at the church gates, or in the roads, using ropes or ladders or carts, or by forming a chain of clasped hands, and they had to stand treat before being allowed to proceed. A good-hearted bridegroom welcomed such interruptions and gladly paid toll on that great day.

At funerals or "burrins," as they were always called, a friend went round "bidding" relatives and friends to attend, and such an invitation was a serious command. As the mourners entered the house of the dead, they placed one shilling or more on a tray at the door, and received a piece of "burrin looaf" (sponge or currant cake), and a memorial card. In this way every mourner helped to meet the heavy expenses of a funeral, which have always pressed so heavily on the poor. Even forty years ago a "free burrin" was a very exceptional occurrence, and a tea provided for the mourners after a funeral was a still more uncommon innovation.

A serious belief in witchcraft prevailed until quite recent times. Old John o' Absalom's, who died in 1876, aged 87 years, used to tell how cows were reversed in their "booses" (stalls), how he had seen calves run up the wall and do other impossible antics, when they were under the influence of the dreaded witches.

His son, Thomas, when a boy living at Nichol House, reported one morning that after retiring to rest, he had frequently been troubled by a reputed old witch then living at the top of Trawden, who came to his bedside and said to him, "I'll hev thee, Tommy," although the door never opened to allow her to pass. In great anger he prepared for her next visit by taking a hay fork to his room. When she next appeared he jumped out of bed, raced after her as she moved backwards, and tried to pin her to the door with his fork. The fork stuck fast in the door and left marks which bore witness for many a long year afterwards that he had really tried to fix her, but the clever old witch had passed unharmed through the key-hole.

On one occasion quarrymen returning from Catlow Delph saw an old woman apparently asleep on the grass in Job Lane. They believed that she was a witch and that her spirit was absent on witchcraft bent. Had she been touched, her spirit would not have returned to its mortal frame, so they waited until she showed signs of awakening, when her evil spirit returned to take possession, and then went hurriedly on their way lest her evil eye should light on them.

A man who died about twenty years ago, said that he remembered as a boy playing with several others on Trawden Hill, when they caught a strange cat which had often been seen playing round them. Very cruelly they tied its limbs close to its body, and when quite helpless they bounced it on the ground like a ball. To their surprise it vanished. That same night an old woman who lived in Back Lane and was bed-ridden was found before morning to have one leg badly broken. It confirmed the general opinion that she was a witch.

Many circumstantial accounts have been given of spirits appearing at the moment when they left the body at death, but these are somewhat commonplace.

It was a common belief in Winewall that at "Old Christmas" night all the cattle in the laithes bowed their heads at midnight, a sure sign that on that night long long ago Christ was born and they did Him reverence. This was also confirmed by the fact that at Stunstead Hall there was a tree which blossomed in full on that self same night. The fact was said to be indisputable, because many people had stayed up all that night and seen it.

"Mischief Night" was a relic of the old English May Day frolics. It was the last night in April, and young people then assumed that they had a free licence for all kinds of pranks. People remember yet when a cart was placed on the roof of a barn at Winewall. A wheelbarrow on the top of a house or barn on the first morning in May was not an uncommon sight. On a large scale, gates were once removed from their hinges and stacked in a distant field not far from The Rough. Carts were often placed in exceptional positions, one being once run into the pool at the bottom of Lumb Spout. Poultry huts had sometimes been moved across a field.

Even the girls had their milder frolics, by closing the stiles with stones, by piling stones at the house doors, and by removing the top slab from the "benk," which stood at the door of most cottages. In the early evening one of them would ask at a cottage door, " Do you want any haver bread (oatcake)?" Meanwhile her companions filled the opening between door and framework with shells of mussels or cockles, and as the door was pulled back there was a loud crash.

Football matches were very popular, not so frequent, but more exacting than the modern type, because every man had to join the game. The game was played between all the men of Trawden or Winewall, and the men of Colne, or Colne Waterside. The ball was kicked off at some place midway between the townships, say at Cowfield or Doughty, and each party tried to get it to their own place. There were no rules of the game, and no time limit. The play was very rough at times, bruises and serious wounds being made, while when they came to the river it was not unusual for men to be soused in the water. At one such game, when Big Joany had kicked off at Cowfield on Christmas Day, the play lasted till evening, and had ultimately reached the Trawden Valley near the watercourse. Then did Joany lift the ball above his head, and dare anyone to touch him or the ball, as he carried it off in triumph to Trawden.

The verses called "Blueberry Cake," which will be given later, were said to have been written as a sequel to this famous football match.

An exactly similar incident is said to have happened at the end of a match between Winewall and Waterside, when old John Mitchell, an exceptionally strong man, was the hero of the day.

Up to forty years ago, on account of the bad country roads, it was the custom to carry quicklime from Lothersdale to the outlying farms on " lime galls." These were small horses about 14 hands high, and each carried three hundredweights, placed in two panniers. A long string of twenty of these horses formed a striking picture as they marched in single file.

A belief in the magical power of gipsies once led to a Thornedge farmer having the confidence trick played on him. Gipsies camping on the waste ground in Wycollar Lane convinced him, by a preliminary trial on a small scale, that copper or silver could be changed into gold, if it was wrapped up by an old woman of their tribe, charmed by her, and then hidden for three days. They persuaded him to repeat the trial with one hundred sovereigns. An essential condition was that he must not come near, nor even look towards the camp for the space of three days. In the night they departed, but poor Johnnie faithfully observed the required conditions, thereby fully earning the name his neighbours gave him for the rest of his life of "Gipsy Johnnie."

People speak yet of Christmas boxes, but long ago the usual presents which a parent gave to his children were small black or tin boxes, costing about a penny each, and these were used to hold pins. The children went to the shopkeeper and said, "Pray you now a row of pins," and he would give a row of pins to every child who asked for this Christmas present. Without toys, they used these pins for several games. In one game a girl covered both ends, and asked another to guess which was head or point. In another guessing game the pin was held in the closed fist, while the holder said "Nip o' butter for a pin, which hand is the butter in?" If guessed correctly the guesser took the pin, but if wrong she lost one.

NICKNAMES.

When there were several individuals owning the same Christian name and surname it was a mental relief and almost a necessity to use some other distinguishing appellation, as in the case already given of Old John, Young John, Little John. Similarly "Little Will," who inherited Trawden Hall, was so called because his father was Young

Will, the son of Old Will. The commonest method was to name a boy as his father's son. Thus if the father was Jack and the son Jem, the son was naturally called Jem o' Jack's.

Some years ago in Liverpool I met an old man named Harrison on a business matter, who had no possible chance of knowing me or my birthplace. Suddenly he asked, "You are not a Liverpool man, but Lancashire?" I agreed. Then his next question was surprising. "Did you ever know Jack o' th' old Mon's?" My reply at once was, "No, he was before my time, but I knew Jane o' Bill's o' Jack's o' th' Old Mon's very well."

It subsequently appeared that Mr. Harrison was the son of a former master of the Colne Grammar School, and in his old age there was no place or topic so interesting to him as that of Bonnie Colne and the neighbourhood, and the people who had lived there.

Thirty years ago Jack Hartley named eight men then living in Trawden who had the same name of John Hartley. Quite recently his son was able to give me the names of seven of these men, as follows :— Jack Hartley, John o' Steens, Jack o' Moys, Potter, Jack Owget, Jack o' Doads, and Scarman.

If a man lived to be over fifty years of age, it was fairly certain that he would receive the prefix "Old," unless some other more striking title had been previously attached to him. A farmer was sometimes named from his farm. Farmer Jack at the Rings Farm was called "Jack at Rings." Similarly, Jack at Lumb Laithe, Hargreaves at Wanlass.

A little incident often caused a name to be attached to a man for life. A boy who volunteered to be a witness when others were caught for stealing potatoes, was called "Witness" for the rest of his life.

When trees were being cut down, a boy seized an axe lying near and swung it round saying, "Let me be the felly." Unfortunately he chopped off his brother Andrew's finger. In later years few people could have recognised William Lee so quickly as by his other name of "Felly Lee."

Billie Boy and Little Tom retained these childish names although both developed into big strong men. In the case of the second man the advantage of the nickname is apparent, because there were two

54

other men, living at the same time, who had exactly the same name, Thomas Shaw, and they all lived near each other at the Top of Trawden.

The system of nicknames is of great antiquity. In 1558, a certain John Hartley was better known as Pynns, and another man was referred to as Parkyn. An important resident in those days called Roger Hartley was always described as Little Hogge.

Nicknames were sometimes abhorred, but in other cases were a source of gratification to their owners. This uncertainty, however, makes me very chary of giving all the names and details collected under this heading. Sometimes a man was well pleised with his additional name, but the very mention of such a name would rouse another man to a violent passion. In the latter case the knowledge was used by his enemies or by mischievous boys who wished to tantalise him.

About eighty years ago this led to a tragic incident. There was then living in Hollin Hall a man who utterly detested his nickname. On dark evenings, boys would shout out his name near his house and he would jump up and race after them, sparing no effort to catch and punish them. But they were agile and swift footed and enjoyed teasing him. They also increased his fury by waiting in the road at intervals until he nearly reached them, but when almost in his grasp they quickly sped away. One evening in desperation he shouted to them that he had a loaded gun, and if anyone troubled him again in a similar manner he would shoot them. There was quietness in the lane that night, but on the following evening he had the same provocation. Seizing his gun with murderous intent he ran swiftly after them. The boys ran along Hollin Hall over the slope of Cock Hill, but as he approached the ridge he saw one waiting in the middle of the road evidently playing the same old game. After a warning shout, he shot, and the boy rolled over, dead. He slowly returned home to tell his anxious wife what he had done. In deep distress, realising the consequences, she suggested that they should dig a grave outside, bury the body, and try by silence to evade the deserved punishment. At the back of the house they dug a cavity and fetched the body to bury. Her womanly curiosity, however, cried for the recognition of the lad, so a light was fetched, when, to their amazement, it was found that the body was made of straw.

Ten years after I heard this story, it was repeated in every detail by Bill o' John's (William Shaw), who had been absent from Trawden for over twenty years, but had returned to live in Winewall.

CHAPTER IX.

POETS AND POETRY.

The conditions of life in Trawden have never been conducive to the growth of a leisured class capable of attaining literary ability of a high order. There have been no poets of eminence who showed marked ability, because none of them was privileged to enjoy the advantages of a good education and make the acquaintance of the vast treasures of English prose and poetry which are available to every literary student. Lacking the knowledge of the possible variations in accent, metre, and rhythm, they enjoyed the expression of their thoughts in simple rhymed verses, written to commemorate some striking local event. They resemble the old ballads made to be sung at feasts or fairs or on special occasions and remembered for long periods even by people who could not read.

The earliest poems that I have come across are contained in a little book called, "Miscellaneous Poems," or "The Good Man's Companion," composed by James Driver, who had lived in Trawden as a boy, but removed in later years to Hyde, in Cheshire. His pride in his poetical gift was evidently reasonable, because the copy, lent me by his grandson, Vincent Driver, shows that this book had passed through nine editions. It begins :—

> This little book does bear the test
>   When it's severely tried;
> It took its stand among the best,
>   Its fame is spreading wide.
>
> It sweetly chimes in every part
>   Like music to the ear:
> It melts the hardness of the heart,
>   And makes them shed a tear.

In an introductory poem he tells how nine years ago he began to write a book, but before it was half way done, 'twas thrown into a nook. Then as he lay on his bed the inspiration came, poetic force awakened him, touched his organ string, and he began a book to make for people now to sing. He describes how he intends it to be both true and kind and that the scriptures shall always be his guide. He concludes this poem by hoping that after his spirit has taken its flight "this book may then be shining bright and spread the nation round."

The most interesting selection describes a walk from **Hollin Hall** along **Slack** Bottoms to Hoyle.

THE BOY'S RAMBLE IN THE WOODS.

In Trawden township I was born,
  Near to the Hollin Hall;
'Twas there my father cut the corn
  When I was very small.

There did I suck my mother's breast—
  Her love to me was deep;
She took me in her arms to rest
  And put me, then, to sleep.

She combed my hair and made it smooth,
  And washed my hands and feet;
When I was sick she did me soothe,
  To cause me not to weep.

Her loving thought and tender care
  For me the table spread,
Enough there was and some to spare,
  For I was richly fed.

Year after year her willing feet
  Unto my help they ran;
She clothed me well and made me meat.
  Called me her little man.

One summer's day I took a rove
  Across you rosy plain;
I sat me down beneath the grove
  To shelter from the rain.

There at my feet a shining grub,
  The rainbow arch was bright;
The wren did sing upon a shrub
  And filled me with delight.

Soon did the clouds begin to break,
  The rain was swept away;
The sun shone bright across the lake,
  Then all was calm and gay.

I turned me round and plucked a rose—
  Its beauty pleased me well —
And when I put it to my nose
  It gave a pleasant smell.

The throstle made the woods to ring,
  Its notes did swell and rise;
The blackbird she did sweetly sing,
  They filled me with surprise.

The skylark rose and sung on high—
  How neat she spread her wing—
Where e'er I looked or turned mine eye
  The birds did sweetly sing.

There, at the bottom of the hill,
  The apple trees did stand;
I took a walk there at my will,
  To see a sight so grand.

The plums and cherries there did hing,
  At them I gazed awhile;
I turned and saw the apples swing,
  The sight it made me smile.

I walked outside the orchard wall,
  Near to the kitchen door;
There, ducks and hens, both great and small,
  Were feeding from the floor.

Before the door the plum tree stood,
  Across the wall it spread;
On it were plums, both ripe and good,
  And some were very red.

The peacock walked across the yard,
  Majestic was his form;
He took his stand there, as a guard,
  To keep the rest from harm.

Two pretty maids came out to me,
  Their words were soft and kind;
They said that I might pluck the tree,
  If that would please my mind.

Those words came sweetly to my breast,
  Just suited to my will;
I climbed the tree and plucked the best—
  I did my bishop fill.

Then, with my plums I ran with haste
  Across you pleasant wood;
That I might let my mother taste,
  To feel how sweet and good.

Across the room to me she run,
  And asked me where I'd been;
Before I'd got my story done
  The truth was fully seen.

The tears then dropped down from her eyes,
  Her words were sweet and mild;
She prayed that God would keep me wise,
  A good and happy child.

She gave to me a raisin cake,
  And put me then to bed—
I write this poem for other's sake,
  So may the truth be spread.

My summer's walk filled me with joy,
  Its pleasure was my wage;
I was but then a little boy,
  About nine years of age.

Most of his poems are serious, reflecting a hard-working life with little leisure and with few comforts or luxuries, while a deeply religious vein runs through them. In "Manhood and Old Age" he compares his weakness and illness due to age with the great strength and activity of his youth.

"The Author's Lamentation" begins,

> I'd nineteen children born to me—
> A great and mighty work, you see,
> To pay expenses great and small,
> The doctor's bills, and rent, and all.

Continuing, he tells of the work and worries in rearing them, and ends by relating his own sufferings due to old age. In "The Old

Poet's Lot," he says that he gets his living by selling his books, that he wanders alone far from home, my books by my side, my staff in my hand, my bill I do read when I sit or stand.

His latest poems describe the battles of Alma and Inkerman, both fought in 1854.

A typical popular ballad, written in anapaestic feet instead of the common ballad measure, is the one called Bloorberry Cake or Blueberry Cake. The author is anonymous, and it has been published both in the dialect and in the modern English.

> On the sixth day of August, as I have heard say,
> All the people left Trawden on that very day;
> With large packs on their backs they came marching through Colne—
> There was a cheap trip on to Liverpool town.
>
> When they got to the station there were folks from all sides—
> Wycollar, Trawden, and Colne Waterside;—
> Such thrusting and crushing—it was like a Wake—
> For no one could stir for the Blueberry Cake.
>
> When they got in the train a man from Winewall
> Said to Old Jeffry, " This engine will stall!
> As sure as we're going we shall have a mistake,
> There is such a great weight on of Blueberry Cake."
>
> They were Umpleby, and Cops, and lots of them more,
> Had as much Blueberry Cake as would fill half-a-score;
> With bottles of porter their sides did shake,
> Besides some large bundles of Blueberry Cake.
>
> When the train it did land and the people got out,
> Jack o' th' Old Mon's set up a great shout;
> The porters did laugh till their sides did shake,
> To see such large bundles of Blueberry Cake.
>
> To see Nelson's Monument off they did run,
> Liverpool people did laugh at the fun,
> To see them stand round, like asses and apes,
> Munching and chewing their Blueberry Cakes.
>
> Then down to the docks in scores they did run,
> And o'er to New Brighton to see the big gun;
> Said Tommy o' Mary's, " My stomach it aches,
> I'm sea sick with eating those Blueberry Cakes."
>
> Said Billy o' Hobs, " I'm thinking o' th' train,
> Let's go back into England, and homeward again "
> So then off they did sail, to the station they went,
> And got back to Colne, which was their intent.
>
> They trudged into Trawden, all sorts, young and old,
> Being half starved to death, both weary and cold;
> Then up spoke Daywark, and lots of them more
> Said. " I'll ne'er cross the sea while I live any more."

There was a reply to the above song written in the same poetical measure by another anonymous author.

A noted character in Winewall fifty years ago was Hartley Stansfield, Hartley o' Anns. He was a very eccentric man, who gathered fresh eggs from the farmers and carried them in baskets to sell in Burnley. Once his baskets had been new, but it was in the far distant past, and in his later years they were tied with string in many places, thus presenting a very bizarre appearance. His clothes also had undergone such an extensive series of patchings that it was difficult to tell which was original material and which was of later age.

I am indebted to Mr. James Hartley, of Bank Street, Trawden, who supplied me with ten printed poems or ballads written by Hartley o' Anns. Both matter and metre are rather disappointing, but when read aloud to other people they produce the same lively interest that old ballads have always done. One song is about a foot race in 1860 won by Little Colne. Another celebrates the marriage of the Prince of Wales in 1863. Another describes the tragedy at Black Lane Ends in 1862. In "Shillings and Pence," and in "My Baskets," he describes his own personal appearance and his occupation and the remarks people make about him as he walks along, with evident pride.

Another poet of Winewall, whose name, unfortunately, has been forgotten, wrote the famous Christian Hymn, reciting the birth and life, the crucifixion and resurrection of our Lord Jesus Christ. It has been sung for many years at Christmas time as a carol. There are in all twenty-four verses, but only the following are usually sung :—

> Ye mortals all, of high and low degree
> Draw near awhile, and listen unto me
> Whilst I unfold these lines which here you find:
> They were composed to keep us fresh in mind.
>
> Of what our Gracious God for us hath done.
> By sending here His dear beloved Son;
> While thousands on the brink of ruin lay,
> He sent His Son, our sinful debts to pay.
>
> Let us observe this Prince of lowly birth,
> When he at first descended here on earth,
> Was by His mother in a manger laid,
> Who, when she bore Him, was in truth a maid.
>
> This Sweet Babe's birth both far and near did ring,
> Reaching the ears of Herod, the great king;
> That mighty monarch, for to stir up strife,
> Resolved to take away His tender life.
>
> Soon we must die, and Christ our Judge will be,
> To serve our Maker let us all agree,
> That He may say Who sits upon the throne,
> "Come saints, I died for you: you are My own."

The new road connecting Trawden to Cottontree was built in 1870, and the notable events of that year caused Mr. Jack Hartley, of Lane House, to write the best dialect verses that I have yet seen.

Just listen, I'll tell you what's gooan 'afore t' Board,
Ther's bin a good deal o' bother abaat this Trawden new rooad,
But naah it's baan on throo malice and spite,
They nother care for William o' Aaron's, Tom at Wanless, nor Joe Wright.

Joe Bannister they say he is the best man,
To help on this rooad he does all he can,
Mr. Shaw is opposed to it and lots on 'em more,
And what they intend is to keep Trawden poor.

Jimmy Taylor went daan one day for to look,
He said it must go on awther by hook or by crook,
But Tom at Nook an' Jam Whalley they sooin fan him aat,
He'd turn raand for moost brass withaat ony daat.

In the month of October when fooek pay their rent,
Some a' th' upper taan farmers to Barrowford went,
I pray you excuse me for naming this trick,
For at this time the new road wi Barrowford men it did stick.

John Redman to his landlord coom aat varrie broad,
He said, "All yer tenants are aggean this new rooad,
There's Tom o' Jems, an Jack o' Moys, aar John an' Cob wife,
If this new rooad gooes on they caant pay t' rent for ther life."

Jim o Becker's said to Gage, "I dar bet mi life,
If this new rooad gooes on we's booath get a wife.
We'll stand boldly up to 'em and make ther hearts quake,
For I know if we get them they'll keep us to lake."

John o' Moses Shays says he's the mayor o' this taan,
If this rooad gooes on old Fanny shall hev a new gaan,
Or ony thing else that he can affooard.
An' they'll walk arm-i'-arm daan this Trawden new rooad.

Billy Marsden's a man that hesent much chatter,
He's opposed to the rooad but he's fair on for watter,
So they've tried up o' t' Th'Hoil, up o' t' moor, an Paul bank,
But Paul says they monnot hev it, he wants it all for his tank.

He says they monnot tak it nor alter its cooarse,
But Local Board thinks it's best spot, so they'll tak it by fooarce
An Birtwistle's men 's bin an mapped it all aat,
So there'll be booath rooad and watter withaat ony daat.

Holgate and Likely are top full o' talk,
They say daan this new rooad they nivver will walk,
They say if it gooas on it will give Trawden a stab,
It will nivver do ony good, it will be covered wi a scab.

Old Rip coals wi a barrow, he looks i' good blow,
Abaat this new rooad he's allas wantin' to know,
He says if it gooas on he will alter his plan
And put daan a coil pit as fast as he can.

There's one William Midgley he's bin chairman for t' Booard,
Just naah he's turned agean this Trawden new rooad,
For 't time is coming on when he'll hev to pay,
So he's doin all he can to stop it they say.

So naah to conclude and finish my rime,
I could a mentioned moor names if od only had time,
But the rooad naah is letten, if you want setting on,
Yo mon goa to Bill Clough, he will pay like a mon.

John Bannister, of Carr View, spent many happy hours in making
rhymes on topical subjects. When street lighting was initiated in
Trawden it was thought to be a worthy occasion for a grand procession

of school children, a free tea ior old folks, and a concert by the massed village choirs in the Primitive Methodist Chapel.   He thought that celebration called for a poetic effusion to emphasise the advantages of having progressive local rulers.   One of the most enthusiastic members of the Local Board at that time was Mr. Hartley Pilling, who invariably enlivened its proceedings, so he is named in these lines.

ONWARD IS OUR MOTTO.

Onward, oh, onward, we must be pressing,
Never stand still but always progressing.
Better and plainer you would it find,
If I could give names I have in my mind.

A few improvements I now will relate,
But whatever I do the truth I must state,
When Trawden new road was going to be made,
Mountains of obstacles you know were then laid.

We shall have to fight if we ever contend,
Suffering humanity we try to mend,
For some will obstruct all ever they can
Because they've not got the mind of a man.

Oh, some are so dull and can't be made see,
The good in the future it's sure to be.
Winewall and Wycollar tried with their might
To stop the new road but gave up the fight.

For some are so weak but so easily led.
One man stood up and tauntingly said,
This road must be made, by hook or by crook,
You may hear men talk, to their ways you must look.

A Liverpool trial was caused. but they lost,
We all have to share in the hundreds it cost.
All now are agreed and have frankly confessed
That with the new road we now all are blessed.

It has eased the rates, we now can see profit,
And some can learn best when it touches the pocket.
Now the next best thing all the women can tell,
They have plenty at home without ing to the well.

It once used to be, "Come, fetch me some watter."
You know then it caused a great deal of chatter.
But if to top of Trawden the water they bring,
Their praises we always will endeavour to sing.

The telegraph too with business so quick,
When improvements we get, to them we must stick.
Then there are two letter boxes put in the wall,
No selfish motive but benefits for all.

And for the above we all ought to praise
One who worked hard and spent many days.
Then also the gas which gives us good light,
At home and in mills both morning and night.

Also the lamp posts that have long been pending,
Yea, three or four years some's been contending.
We've got them at last, to all it is nice,
Sixpence per thousand, it's lowered the price.

The old and the young, how pleased they will be.
When they go round the gas lights to see,
October eighteenth, I think we shall see
All will be lit up, and opened with tea.

A man came forward with some agitation,
Let's all try to make a great demonstration.
He then did propose, some thought he was bold,
A regular good tea for all that were old.

" As first on the list I'll give ten shillings,"
His name is well known to be Mr. Pilling.
It soon was resolved to make a subscription,
And ensure a reality and not a mere fiction.

So sixty and over had all to be free.
Yes, all to enjoy a knife and fork tea.
The question came next and what for the young,
Oh, all under twelve, free coffee and bun.

There's lots of things more that I might have said,
But to uneasiness it might have led.
Just a few things I think I will mention,
To create bad feelings I have no intention.

By a Local Board we reckon to be ruled,
But things would be better if we were well schooled.
To have a good Board look to selection
By choosing good men at every election.

The Board is just what we make it to be,
So people of Trawden to this we must see.
I want you to see that we cannot afford
To let Mr. Pilling go out of the Board.

There's lots of men say he is the best man,
So let us all do whatever we can.
And when the time comes, he'll want our support,
And this we can do when we've got to vote.

Few men can you find that are able and willing,
With time to devote as does Mr. Pilling.
The time may come round when more can be said,
I'll close for the present, I'm now off to bed.

The late Mr. W. B. White, of Colne, began one of his poems
with the following verse :—

Well done thou grand old Trawden, at the foot of Boulsworth Hill,
Where men have lived and still do live possessed of mind and will;
Men who themselves have rais-ed to the pinnacle of wealth and fame,
Yet in humble personal appearance they keep almost the same.

Lastly come the poems of the present poet and writer of Trawden,
Joseph Hartley, of Carr View, better known perhaps as a popular
ventriloquist, but also a writer of verses equal to or surpassing in quality
the best attempts previously quoted.   He has been a prolific writer
and during the recent Great War several of his poems were published
and sold to raise funds for the wounded soldiers and sailors.   In this
way he tried to give patriotic service to his country in the best way
open to him.   He has many choice musical poems in his selection as
will be seen below.

GOOD OLD TRAWDEN.

Hurrah for good old Trawden,
No tongue can tell its worth,
This blessed place of childhood
That gave us sacred birth.

63

Within its cherished boundaries,
On hill, in vale or dale,
With tokens of glad rapture,
Each beauty spot we hail.

'Tis joy for us to wander
Beneath its shady trees.
In moorland fields to ramble
Mid soft refreshing breeze.

The dear old church, quite stately,
Stands in her lofty place,
Just like some glorious beacon,
This edifice of grace.

God bless our native village,
Each youth and maiden fair.
The aged and the children,
To them no place so rare.

For oh, what joy and gladness,
Each heart sweet music sings,
And all with sweetest fondness.
To good old Trawden cling.

WYCOLLAR.

Oh Wycollar, fair Wycollar, thy name with joy we greet,
Oh Wycollar, fair Wycollar, with air so pure and sweet.
We love to wander by the brook that ripples in the breeze;
We love to spend an hour or two beneath the shady trees.

Oh Wycollar, fair Wycollar, we raise our voice and sing.
Oh Wycollar, fair Wycollar, we make the woodlands ring.
We all will sing a happy song, sing as we ramble on,
Begone dull care and all prepare to join us in our song.

Oh Wycollar, sweet Wycollar. the happy hours we spend.
Oh Wycollar, sweet Wycollar, that makes our pleasures blend,
Thy beauty seems for ever fresh, no matter where we glance
In rippling brook or ingle nook, it makes our glad heart dance.

Oh Wycollar, fair Wycollar, with fields and meadows green,
Oh Wycollar, fair Wycollar, we sing a joyous theme.
We sing to all the trees and flowers and every bursting bud,
We sing again a loud hurrah, hurrah, Wycollar Wood.

THE CUCKOO.

List and hear, list and hear, list to the cuckoo's song.
Borne, borne on the breeze, over the rustling trees.
Over the vale and the hill and the lane,
List to its joyous and sweet refrain,
        Sing it again to me,
Sing my little bird, sing my pretty bird, sing.

Hark again, hark again, list to its glorious note.
Hark, hark, how they float, over the silent moat
Over the meadow the field and the plain,
List to its joyous and sweet refrain,
        Sing it again to me,
Sing my little bird, sing my pretty bird, sing.

TO A NEW BORN BABE.

(Written on the morning of his child's birth.)

O thou sweet and heavenly dewdrop,
Gift of God sent from above,
Thine to make hearts intermingle,
With more gracious fervent love.

64

The Bannister family in the back yard of their home, 31 Church Street, Trawden about 1897. Mother and father, Jane and David, had 8 sons and 3 daughters. Fred, author of this book, has his hand on his mother's shoulder. The photo was taken by Barcroft and Crabtree, who had studios in Burnley, Nelson and Bacup.

Lowlands Well, Wycoller is fed from a spring, the main source of drinking water for the villagers before piped water came. This farmer's wife in her working clogs is getting her family's water. The groove in the large stone is to hold a wooden cover for the water, thus preventing animals from using it, and leaves fouling it.

Imagine riding one of these up brew in Trawden. Brothers Fred (right) and Hartley
Bannister proudly display their new safety cycles about 1888 in a photographer's
studio. Note the cycles' solid wheels, the brake on the front wheel only and the foot
rests on the front forks, which were for resting the rider's feet when riding down hill,
for the cycles had a fixed gear

Trawden residents William and his sister Martha Ellen out for a spin about 1910.

Brothers Fred (left) and Will Bannister find time for a stroll with Rev. James Walton about 1906, which is when he married into the Bannister family. Trawdener James was a Methodist minister and went on missionary work with his new wife to Africa.

A photo taken by Bath Hartley, who had a studio in Trawden, at Dyke Farm about 1893. A small farm would support a large family and some hired labour.

Another Bath Hartley photo of a group of Trawdeners out for a walk on t'tops one Sunday before the turn of the century.

The trustees of Skipton Road Methodist Chapel, Trawden, about 1919. All good men and true. The chapel was demolished about 1951.

The first Sunday in August, about 1905. The Skipton Road Chapel Anniversary Sunday — "*t'Sermons*". Hartley Bannister is playing the bass fiddle. There's not a bare head to be seen.

Scholars at the Trawden Council School about 1900. Many of these lads and lasses would live their lives in the village and have children proud of their Trawden roots.

Members of the Trawden Wesleyan Chapel in their concert dresses in the early days of the century. The *"bobby"* doesn't look very tall, so he was probably a character in the play being performed.

Dating from prehistoric times, this Wycoller bridge is an example of a clam (i.e. single-span) bridge. Since Bert Hindle took this photograph the bridge has been broken by flood waters.

A young man surveys the Forest of Trawden from the top of Boulsworth, the highest point in the Forest. The photo was probably taken by Trawdener Charlie Green in the 1920's. He was related to this book's author.

Charlie Green took this photo of members of the Colne Natural History Society preparing to ascend Boulsworth in September 1927.

A photo taken in Wycoller in 1926, probably by Charlie Green. The farmer's work continues whilst a party of visitors looks around the village.

A view of Wycoller showing the pack-horse bridge. The village has always been a favourite picnic place for visitors from nearby towns, though the ducks show that there was a working farm nearby. The bridge carried the main road from Colne to Haworth in the days of handloom weaving.

Great the power which thou possesseth,
Helpless though thy frame may be,
There is more in thy frail body,
Than the human eye can see.

For thou art by God created,
Precious gem thou art so fair,
Gifts like thee we all should cherish,
More than diamonds rich and rare.

As we scan thy tiny features,
Some new beauty we behold,
As some pure unconscious action,
Thy sweet tissues doth unfold.

Heaven-sent sweet little rosebud,
May thy beauty never fade,
But thy being on earth bring blessing,
Pure and innocent sweet babe.

Mr. J. Hartley has also written a dialect musical sketch, **entitled**
"Lumb Laithe," with scenes laid at Lumb Laithe farm house **and in**
Wycollar woods. On several occasions this sketch has been **performed**
locally with quite remarkable success.

CHAPTER X.

PLACE NAMES AND DIALECT WORDS.

A study of the place names in Trawden Forest cannot fail to recall some of its past history and provide interesting material on which the imagination may work. Someone in the past had a reason for giving to each place its own peculiar name, and it may be possible to discover or suggest the reasons for some of these names.

It must not be forgotten that until very recent times it was the spoken word that was important and not the written or printed word. Names were always handed down from father to son as spoken words not written ones. If some individual was careless in speech, a word might be changed if it was not frequently used, so that we cannot always tell what its original form or meaning may be.

The first Ordnance Survey maps of this district were made in 1844, when the Survey Officers, with sappers and miners, made a great camp on Boulsworth, and the names inserted on those maps were then obtained from the landowners or tenants. Previous to this survey the only means of fixing the names was by title deeds which might remain unaltered for many years while the spoken word would change. The most genuine word, therefore, whether place name or dialect word, is the original spoken word and not the written word.

The selection of names given is not exhaustive. On some farms every field and meadow has its own peculiar name, but these names are known only by the landlords.

The name of Trawden itself has been the subject of much conjecture. The learned historian of Craven and Whalley, Dr. Whittaker, said it was probably derived from Troughden, the hollow or excavated valley, but there is no certainty for this derivation. In the early records it is variously spelled as Trochdene, Troudene, Trouden, Trogden, Troveden, Troweden. Similarly the name of Winewall is given as Wynewelle, Wynwall, Wynewall, and Wycollar as Wicoler, Wycoller, Wykecollar, and so on. The clerical writers of those days always had the privilege of spelling the words as they pleased, but the sounds of these names have probably changed very little from the earliest times. No one can say with certainty what these words originally described. It was called a forest because it was first used as a

66

hunting forest by the lord of the manor. It has always consisted of mixed grasslands and woods and never been a completely wooded district.

The Deerstones, Deerstones Moor, Staghole (now called Seg-hole), Cathole Clough, tell us of hunting days one thousand years ago. What were the deeds that made these places famous? Carry Heys, the edge of the marshy place; Prospect House, overlooking the hamlet with Larkhill near to it; Backside Farm, on the slope away from Colne; the Moss, Meadow Bottoms, Naze End, Midge Hole, Green-bank; Alderhurst and Alderbarrow, the hill and the barrow near the alder trees; Oakenbank, The Rough, Great Hill, Gillford Clough, Thorn Edge, all suggest their origin long ago.

Stunstead, the farm or holding near the stones, is descriptive and appropriate because the best quarries have always been there or on the same ridge in Winewall hamlet itself, but in 1508 there was a Dunt-houstead which may be the original name. The peculiar name of Lane-house or Lanehouse Lane, one of the most important roads in Trawden, calls for notice. In 1670 Lane occurs alone as a place name where Widow Hartley lived. Probably there was some important house in the Lane between Trawden and the Upper Town. Then as houses were built, it became known as Lanehouse, and quite recently the longer name has been adopted.

The names of Hollin Hall and Antley may have been given by the earliest settlers who came there from Hollings and Antley near Accrington, about the time that the Cunliffes of Hollings and Cunliffe settled at Wycollar Hall.

Above Hollin Hall the outlying cottages and farm houses form the Upper Town. In this area, Th' Hoil, or Hoyle, formed an import-ant hamlet in itself, having a population of over 100 souls, whereas now it consists of only two farmhouses.

The main hamlet must always have been from Trawden Hall along the sloping ground still called Trawden Hill, to the bottom, which was the Town Gate Bottom. This was on the chief highway to Colne through which most of the trade would naturally pass.

Church Street, so called since the church was built, was formerly Smithy Lane, because the blacksmith's shop was there. This is one of the oldest roads, being named in 1510, as the high road,between Emmut Brig and Shelfield.

Joining the Towngate to Smitny Lane was Back Lane, evidently a later road, and ending in Clogg Heads. Below these houses come "the streets," built by one of the Midgleys of Stunstead Hall. Top Street is the highest, Mill Street was opposite the old corn mill, Low Street is a depression from the main road, while Chapel Street contains the houses in which both Wesleyans and Primitive Methodists held their initial cottage services.

Dialect Words.

Dialects have often been regarded as vulgar corruptions of the English language, but this is a mistaken notion. When few people had the opportunity of learning to read or write, book English was unknown, and the genuine local language was a separate and distinct tongue handed down from parents to children, generation after generation, with little change in pronunciation or extension of vocabulary.

Owing to its seclusion Trawden has retained many survivals of an earlier speech which, although now obsolete, were formerly regarded as current literary English. This was impressed on me during a course of study at Birmingham University, of the poems of Lawrence Minot, who lived about 1340. They are difficult to read because of the number of obsolete words they contain. Recognising many of them as dialect words, I made a long list and handed it to the English Professor with a note that 'these were still living words in frequent use in my native village. Once when I used the word "mire" unconsciously, my companion asked me sarcastically whether I was trying to be Shakespearian, Scriptural or pedantic. This word, however, is the usual Trawden word for mud.

Not very long ago old people used many guttural sounds in their speech, e.g., rough, laugh, dooagh, fought, waugh, frightened, nought, toghee, oghen, almighty.

Then the guttural sound, as in thought, was softened to thowt, and to the modern form of thought. Similarly rochen, became raked, and then reached.

In a large number of words which are spelled with two vowels, modern English has dropped one vowel sound, but both sounds are given in full by the dialect. Thus bread is now called bred, but the dialect word is breead, and in a similar way the full phonetic sounds are given to every letter in pear, dead, death, feast, bean, leave, lead, head, dream, groan, and so on.

In the word "pear," the current pronunciation in northern and southern England shows the same difference.

There are many correct grammatical survivals, e.g., "Ar ta," for "Art thou" is not a corruption. In the verb "To find," a tense is retained which has been dropped in modern English; find, fun, fan, instead of simply find, found.

The majority of real dialect words are survivals of Anglo-Saxon and Middle English speech, and occur frequently in the poems of Spenser and Chaucer. The former poet uses both "a cawf-lick" and a "cat-wesh." Reek, shooen, and een are still Dutch and Icelandic words. "Tay" is the sound given to-day for "tea" in modern French, and it was so called in London in Queen Anne's time; in Winewall they call it "tey," in Cowling they call it "teeah," while in most other places they call it "tee."

Many dialect words have been lost as the older people depart, because the younger ones have never learnt them. To preserve them I have made a dictionary of dialect words. Mr. Barth. Hartley, of Colne, kindly helped me with his collection of dialect words, and when in doubt of the sound or meaning of an uncommon word received from another source I have always been able to refer to the mature opinion of my father, David Bannister. Old people have been astonished frequently to learn that some word which they knew very well was unknown to the younger folk who also spoke the dialect. The words given below are only such as seem to me old expressive words that have almost gone out of use now, or have some peculiar meaning.

Agaitherds, going with someone for company; andclaat, towel; ass, ashes; assoil, ashpit or dustbin; addle, earn; abacko, behind; air-nut, earthnut or pignut; askerd, a water newt; afterins, the last milk from a cow; Ailse, Alice; nattercrop, spider.

Baahen, going; to big, to build; beel, cup handle; benk, a stone slab; bield, shelter; a blow eawt, a feast; booses, cow stalls; brass, money; buffet, stool; breead flake, the rack for oatcake near the ceiling; to bup, to drink (children); bull spink, a dragon fly; belly, stomach or abdomen; beest, the first milk given by a cow after calving; bangs, surpasses; brat, apron; band, twine; better end, the gentry; back end, autumn; bawk, a beam and also to shout loudly; baum tay, herb drink; biting on, a lunch; to give bell tinker, a good thrashing; bobby dazzler, very fine or showy; bowt bread, made by a baker; bodle, a coin worth half a farthing.

Cant, cheerful or capable; to caaer, to sit down; to clam, to be without food; to cooaken, to vomit; capt, surprised; claat, rag or blow; crooiting, complaining; cawf lick, a front tuft of hair that wont lie flt; cat wesh, a pretence at washing; cob, to throw or a lump; in a crack, instantly; to cruddle, to collapse; chaney boned, delicately built; cater corners, cross corners of a square; creease, measles.

Darter, a smart one; daker hen, corn crake; to daahn a warp, to finish it; dicht, dirty; ditherin, shivering; deead hoss, working for what has been paid in advance; dollop, quantity; donned, dressed; doffed, undressed.

Ee and een, eye and eyes; elbow greease, hard work.

Fain, gladly; flay, frighten; faal, ugly or cowardly; fire rahm, mantelpiece; fettle, to put in order; feerful, very; flummoxt, puzzled or upset; to fox, to pretend; fair like, exactly similar.

Gawmless, foolish; gallaces, braces; gerss, grass; gam, brave or fun; gang thi gait, go thy way; gradely, good; guts, bowels; gawm, to understand; ginnel, narrow passage; a good way, a long distance; a gammy leg, a lame leg.

Hoo, she; haersin, harvesting; handkitcher, handkerchief; happen, perhaps; havey cavey, unsteady; host, cough; hiding, thrashing; hummer bee, honey bee; huggin, hip; hushing, scattering money broadcast; haver breead, oatcake.

Iil off, sorry; ittered, covered; iil done to, badly used; a mad ig, a bad temper; jawmb stooens, upright stones; to jowl, to knock; to joss, to push; jimp, neat or tidy; a jiffy, a short time; to jart, to throw with a jerk.

Kaffle, to give up; kittling, kitten; kink host, whooping cough; kittle, tickle; Kersmiss, Christmas; kake, walt, and coggle, all mean to overbalance unawares; kist, chest; kale, turn; keyblow, left-handed; kes, because; to kine back, to reproduce family characteristics.

To like, to love; to leather, to thrash; luvver, chimney; likenst to, been inclined to; as lief as, as soon as; to lake, to play; layken, a plaything (these two words are modern Scandinavian words); looby, an awkward fellow; to go low, to become insane; latching, infectious; to lick, to thrash; to lug, to pull the hair; to let on, to tell a secret; iicker or stunner, an exceptionally good one; lip, impudence; lumpheyd, a dull person; loblolly, an odd man; to lig, to lie down; long length, prostrate; lactra, a clatch of eggs for sitting; lobsceawse, hashed potatoes.

mough, hay in barn; mad, vexed; mell, touch; marrow, one of a pair; maerld warp, a mole; mull, dust; marlacks, tricks or pranks; mee mos, dumb show; moithered, worried or troubled; maddled, confused; maskered, rusty; masht up, exhausted; mooter weft, stolen weft; mard, spoiled child, etc.; to be mood eawt, to be overcome.

Numbers were formerly always reckoned in scores, with the units first, e.g., 25 would be called five and twenty. Nought and naughty had guttural sounds. Nobbut, only; natty, handy; noddle, head; nudge, a dig in the ribs; nattering, to nibble, or to nag.

Oghen, owe; ooined, neglected; oon, oven; oddin abeawt, doing odd jobs; ony bit like, reasonable; ower faced, too much.

Punch, a kick with clogs; pratley, slowly or quietly; pyching, hiding; to powl, to cut hair; possing, ducking; pearked, perched; Kersmiss pot, Christmas present; to penk, to throw; to pail, to thump; payswad, pea pod; pot pooasies, herbs for flavouring; posnet, an iron pan; pricking down music, writing out music; powfagged, moithered or wearied; pine-an, a magpie.

Rig, back; rochen, reached; rive riven, tore torn; riddle, sieve; rant, a spree; rick, smoke; rip, a scamp; ratcher, lie or exaggeration; rooiting, rummaging; rare and weel, rare and strict, etc., was a method of saying very; a rider eawt was a commercial traveller.

To shop, to shake; sad cakes, heavy pastry; to settle, to lower the price; to scrike, to scream; sneck, door latch; slat or splat, splashed; skellered, warped; a sooap, a small quantity of liquid; shebster, a starling; stee, a ladder; stail, a broom stick handle; to sile, to strain;

to sipe, to drain; to stick, to stab; shooen, shoes or boots; soas, to scold; snod, smooth; starving never means hungry but very cold; to be set up, to be pleased; to stun on, to depend on; a shut, a window sash; sleeat, to set dogs on; on t' strap, credit; to scutter, to run; sucked in, deceived; to be slippy, to be quick; to shoo hens, to drive them; sidation, a clearance; a sis, a snack; spelk, splint of wood; to stut, to stammer; shive, slice; to sken, to squint; snig, eel; shirty, bad tempered; sallit, salad; styther, rather; shinked, cleaned out of marbles; swither, to burn grass.

The word "ta" is generally used for the second person singular, nominative case, and "thee" for the corresponding objective case, although "yaa" is considered to be more respectful to the person addressed. To tine is to shut, so tine t' door to, means shut the door; taen, taken; threeap, to argue; teem, to pour; to think on, to remember; thrang, busy; to tup, to bump; thible, a porridge stick; tooen awf, the one half; thin, drip, gravy, or meat juice; as near as a toucher, as near as possible; thick, friendly; titivate, to dress up; two double, bent double; cannot thoil, cannot bear; tollol, butterfly; to tipe, to strike a ball, etc.

The vowel "u" is a pure vowel sound in the dialect in many ords such as sure, use, picture, although it has been corrupted in modern English. Urchant, hedgehog; to up end, to rear vertically.

Wenley, nearly or almost; wangley or wamley, weak; wheot, hot; witshod, wetfooted; waugh, tasteless; was in the dialect is never used, but were, which is often grammatically incorrect; whol, until; winter edge, clothes horse; wishin, cushion; weel off, wealthy; whick, living; to white, to cut; to wear, to spend; wartey, a working day; wick things, insects; wrang side eawt, ill tempered; wark meant ache, as in tooth wark, head wark, etc.

CHAPTER XI.

WYCOLLAR AND THE CUNLIFFES.

No part of Trawden Forest is more popular than that of Wycollar. The river and road winding from the high moorland along the secluded valley to the richer meadow lands below attract many people on every holiday in the year. The quaint pack horses' bridge below the ruined hall of the Cunliffes, the stone footbridge opposite the hall, the several rustic bridges higher up, all enhance the natural sylvan beauty of the valley. The ruined haunted hall and the traditions of the cock fighting Cunliffe squires provide romantic possibilities for the imaginative writer and two famous novelists have already taken advantage of these possibilities in their books. Charlotte Bronte in "Jane Eyre" is said to have used Wycollar Hall as the Thornfield Hall of her story. Halliwell Sutcliffe has mentioned Wycollar and the Cunliffes in several of his novels.

Like the other hamlets of Trawden and Winewall it was in the first place a hunting forest and then a cattle rearing district or vaccary in charge of cowherds. In the yearly returns of the rents for herbage in 1423, it is stated that £5 13s. 4d. was received from Geoffrey de Hertley and Robert de Hertley for farm of the grass of Overwycolur and Nether-wycolur vaccaries, demised to them by the steward for 10 years, this fifth year. The old rent was £4 10s., equally in two titles.

In the survey of the forests previous to the disafforestation in 1507, there is a record of the vaccaries of Overwycolur and Nether wicoler that late were in farm at £4 13s. 4d. but now letten to farm to Piers Foldes, Pyers Hertley the elder, and other old farmers of the same for £6 by year whereby it is improved yearly 26s. 8d.

Also there is a waste ground called Emottes Moor in the Forest of Trawden, which paid at this day nothing and every man depastureth it that will, which waste ground is granted to Laurence Towneley and to Rauff Askue by copy of Court Roll, and they do pay therefore yearly for evermore twenty shillings.

In 1527 there were six tenants in Wycollar, four of whom had the surname of Hartley, one of Emmott, and one of Foldes.

In 1662, there were seven tenants, the first being named Elizabeth

Cunliffe, widowe, while two of the Winewall tenants of that year are said to have John Cunliffe land.

THE CUNLIFFES.

The present spelling of this name was settled about the time of James 1st, but the name is of Saxon origin, being derived from Cun or Con, meaning to give or grant, and life. Tradition says that a Saxon prince granted lands to one of his followers saying, "I cun you this land to live or support yourself with." This land was in the hundred and parish of Blackburn, in the townships of Billington, Rushton, and Harwood. Near 'Billington between Hollings and Whalley is Cunliffe House and Cunliffe Moor is near. The family suffered from the invasions of Danes and Normans, but most of all from the wars of York and Lancaster. In Henry VII.th's time they mortgaged the estate to a Walmesley and could not redeem the Cunliffe estate so they settled at Hollings. From then the pedigree is clear. In the time of Charles I. they were first on the side of the Parliamentarians, then on the side of the Royalists, so they were plundered and their estate sequestered. Hollings had to be sold and the family removed to Wycollar Hall, an estate which had come to them by a marriage with the Hartley of Wycollar, members of the family of Hartley of Hartley near Whalley.

Wycollar Hall is said to have been built by Piers Hartley in 1550.

The Wycollar Cunliffes were the descendants of the eldest son of the John Cunliffe of Hollings who married the heiress Hartley. From a younger son descend the Cunliffes of Acton Park, Wrexham, the most important living representatives. This younger son, Ellis, first took the Royalist side in the Civil War, but afterwards the Parliamentary side. Sir R. A. Cunliffe, Bart., of Acton Park, died in 1905, and was succeeded by his eldest son, Mr. Foster E. H. Cunliffe, a historian of the last Boer War.

The Cunliffes lived in Wycollar for four generations as country squires noted for their reckless horsemanship and cock fighting propensities. The traditions of their reckless riding up and down the stairs of the Hall, through the valley, and down the breast of Pendle Hill, led naturally to the legend of the spectre horseman given in Harland and Wilkinson's "Traditions of Lancashire." One of them is said to have been so fond of cock fighting that on his death bed, when he was too feeble to raise his head, he had mirrors placed round his bed, so that he might see his favourite birds fight in his bedroom so long as he breathed.

The last Henry Cunliffe of Wycollar was succeeded by his nephew Henry Owen who took the name of Cunliffe when he succeeded to the Wycollar estate.

Henry Owen Cunliffe had a good education at Bolton Abbey and at Oxford. His uncle, who died when he was twenty-two years of age, had left directions that he should come of age when twenty-five years old, but he immediately assumed the position of squire at Wycollar. He was endowed with a fine generous character, and great abilities, but unfortunately had contracted extravagant habits while at college.

He modernised the Hall, made extensive beautiful gardens and grounds, and through keeping a number of horses, sporting, and living extravagantly, his expenditure soon exceeded his income. To increase his resources he commenced to work a colliery and limekilns on his estate, but on both ventures he lost money. Again seeking to retrieve his fortune, in 1902, he left Wycollar and in later years returned thence only twice a year for rents and for grouse shooting, while he lived at Chapel House on the Wharfe, in Craven, which he rented. At Hardcastle, near Pateley Bridge, ten miles away, he leased the Providence lead mine which was said to be very rich in ore, and worked it. It must have been very rich because he was awarded £20,000 from litigation with a neighbouring mine owner.

It is reported that he was plundered by lawyers, agents, and money lenders, and that he borrowed thousands of pounds at the high rate of ten per cent. The income left to him by his uncle was about £700 per year, but by additional purchases and the increase in value of his lands, the rental was raised to £1,700 per year.

Henry Owen Cunliffe corresponded with Sir Foster Cunliffe of Acton Park, respecting their pedigree and was godfather to one of Sir F. Cunliffe's sons. He also supplied the history of the Cunliffe's to Mr. Mathew Gregson of Liverpool, who copied most of the M.S.S. into his "Fragments of the Duchy of Lancaster," as follows :—"Wycollar Hall was built about 1550—1560 and is a spacious well-built house of curious freestone with the outer and partition walls a yard in thickness. The hall is an admirable specimen of Gothic architecture, the arch for the fireplaces, the cove behind, and stone benches round it, supported upon

75

fields, being all of one piece, is considered as beautiful antique masonry, and in good preservation. It has the reputation of being the most ancient hall in this part of the country. It commands a good extent of land in domain, as well as in good farms. Here the family of Cunliffe has remained in quiet and retirement, content with the possessions Providence has allotted to them, and seldom going out into the world. Usually they farmed their own lands and consumed the produce at home. Our ancestors have been fortunate in marrying good fortunes and heiresses, as well as in marrying their daughters with good houses, with fortunes of £300 to £500 apiece as we have vouchers to show.

That they were well respected is proved by their being so continually made guardians to the gentlemen's and yeomen's families in the neighbourhood.

At Wycollar Hall they usually kept open house for the twelve days at Christmas. Their entertainment was in a large hall of curious ashlar work, a long table, plenty of furmenty, like new milk in the morning, made of husked wheat. Boiled and roast beef, with a fat goose and a pudding, with plenty of good beer for dinner. There was also a round-about fire surrounded with stone benches, where the young folk sat and cracked nuts and diverted themselves. In this manner the sons and daughters got matching without going much from home.

In the recesses above the arch of one of the doorways leading to the kitchen and back premises are two small shields having the date 1596 cut in them.''

The last squire, Henry Owen Cunliffe, was the eldest son of Joseph Owen of Sheffield, and Sarah Scargill, and he married, but had no children. His next brother was Captain Joseph Owen, of the 77th Regiment, who never married and was killed when leading a storming party at the siege of Seringapatam in 1799, so the descendants of Charles the third son of Joseph Owen now represent the elder branch of the Cunliffes through the female line. One of his daughters, Miss Mary Cunliffe Owen, was adopted by Mr. H. O. Cunliffe and brought up as heiress at Wycollar. When the lease of Chapel House in Wharfedale expired, they returned to Wycollar Hall and there the last Squire Cunliffe died in 1818.

In Colne Church there is a brass plate on which is written, "Here

lieth the body of Henry Owen Cunliffe, of Wycollar Hall.   Died 8th
November, 1818.   Aged 66 years."

A hatchmen with the Cunliffe arms hangs on the wall of the
chancel on the north side.

After his death his wife and niece were obliged to leave Wycollar
as they could not afford to keep up the necessary establishment.   Mr.
H. O. Cunliffe had spent much money on the place, modernising part
of the Hall, making large gardens, with a pond and greenhouse beyond
the stables, and largely increasing the stabling as he was very fond of
riding and driving.   Down the steep road from the moor he used to
drive a four in hand.   He had also lost much money through mining
and other speculations and had been compelled to mortgage his estates
beyond their value.

The first mortgagee was the Rev. John Oldham the husband of
his wife's sister, who foreclosed but never came to live at the hall nor let
it to anyone else.   The house and grounds were gradually allowed to
fall into a ruinous state.   He had several offers for the place but would
not sell.   Two brothers of Miss Mary Cunliffe Owen, Captain C. Cunliffe Owen, R.N., in 1855, and Mr. Joseph Owen, who had become a
prosperous merchant of Copenhagen, wished to purchase Wycollar, but
Mr. Oldham would not entertain their offers.

On the side opposite to the road, the rising ground was formerly
covered with trees which he allowed to be cut down and sold.   From
the Hall itself he sold the doors and windows, the roof and timber, and
every kind of valuable material.   As stated in a previous chapter of this
history, my grandfather purchased a large quantity of material to build
the cotton factory of Scar Top, at Trawden, the entrance hall, haunted
chamber above it, the massive stone gate pillars, and a quantity of the
ornamental stonework.   This rapidly hastened the decay of the neglected
building but even yet, sufficient remains to make it the most interesting
ruin in this neighbourhood.

Mrs. Cunliffe retired to Cheltenham, and died there in 1831.   Miss
Mary Cunliffe Owen died at Great Shelford, near Cambridge, in 1879.

In 1858, Wycollar estate with others at Laneshawbridge, Winewall and Colne were sold by auction.

In 1872, Major General C. H. Owen, of the Royal Artillery, worked out the Cunliffe ancestral tree, visited Wycollar and district, and wrote a booklet for private circulation, which he revised in 1887. In this publication, kindly lent me by the last owner, he says, "Formerly there was a population of 300 to 400 people in Wycollar, people mostly engaged in handloom weaving, but the adoption of machinery ruined the trade and there are now only about 60 to 70 people and many empty houses. Enough is left of the exterior of the Hall to show that it must formerly have been a comfortable, picturesque and somewhat imposing house for such an out of the way place, but roof, glass from windows, doors, floors, ceiling and other woodwork have been removed. The grand old fireplace is still intact but the removal of the fine porch has also sadly disfigured the front of the house. The porch, which has two storeys and projected from the front wall of the Hall was removed some years ago and is now built against a small factory in the village of Trawden. The doorway is now filled up by a window and above is a bay window which would formerly have been on the same floor as the storey over the old hall."

The coat of arms of the Cunliffes of Hollings and Wycollar consisted of three hares on a shield.

" Foster's Leap " is the name given to two huge boulders nine feet apart, and is so called because a Foster Cunliffe jumped from one to the other.

THE LEGENDS OF WYCOLLAR HALL.

As the Hall stood massive and lonely and empty for over twenty years before it was dismantled, it would naturally be a fearsome place to the timid who passed on the long dark nights, and the excited fancy would easily repeople it with the spirits of the departed Cunliffes. The legends centre round the stories of a spectre horseman and a black lady. In the "Annals of Colne" the former is well described. Dressed in ancient garb, on a horse breathing out fire, he dashes up the road, across the narrow bridge, dismounts at the door of the Hall, makes his way up the broad oak stairs, into one of the rooms from whence dreadful screams as if from a woman are shortly heard. These soon subside into groans after which he reappears, mounts his horse and gallops off. This happens annually on the darkest and stormiest night of the year. He is doomed to pay this visit because he murdered his wife in that room during his earthly existence. On such a night few people venture

78

abroad, but if any perchance should see him they notice that both he and the horse are transparent.

The late Mr. Frank Slater of Colne published the story with some additional details. He says that the Squire had had his very lovely bride crowned Queen of May in fair Wycollar Dene. In the evening he saw her embrace a youth whom he thought was her secret lover, but who was really her brother. In a jealous rage he rushed into her room and struck her dead with the butt of his dog whip. As reason returned, remorse gripped him, so he mounted his swiftest steed, fled away, and was never seen any more. But as a penance his spirit had to return and re-enact the awful deed for many years until atonement had been made.

The story of the Lady in Black, Old Bess, or Black Bess, is given in detail in the "Annals of Colne." There the old lady is described as being clothed from head to foot in black silk, and hence her name. She said nothing but looked anxiously around, and then withdrew quietly, leaving the two frightened lovers who had watched her unmolested. She was the murdered wife of the Spectre Horseman.

The version of the legend which was told to me has not hitherto been published. One of the wild old Cunliffes crossed the Atlantic ocean to visit the slave states of America or the West Indies. There he married a wealthy black lady because he was in sore need of her money. On the return journey with his bride he threw her overboard rather than bring her to Wycollar. Her spirit followed him however, and often used to appear in the old Hall seeking the man who had drowned her. In that version the Spectre Horseman was not mentioned.

Such are the legends of this beautiful Wycollar Dene, but which, if any, had any origin in fact, we have no means of determining, as it is many long years since these spirits were last reported to appear, nor is there anyone living who has seen or heard these restless ghosts.

CHAPTER XII.

THE FOULDS FAMILY OF TRAWDEN HALL.

The most important family in Trawden itself, and the only family of which a long consecutive record can be traced is that of Foulds and Pilling, of Trawden Hall. The founder of the family, and probably the builder of Trawden Hall, or "le mareage house," seems to have been Geoffrey Ffoldes, who is mentioned in the Court Rolls from 1513 to 1568. He had important holdings in Beardshaw Booth, occupied the position of greave frequently, and must have lived to a good old age, at least 75 years, because no one was first admitted as a copyholder until his 21st birthday.

R. S. Pilling, Esq., architect, of Colne, possesses documents dated 1555 referring to this man, and also to his son and heir, James Foulds, in which he is described in 1586 as the late deceased.

There must have been a close relationship between this family and the Foulds' family of Danes House, Burnley, because each had a very similar coat of arms. After considerable research the ancestral tree of the Trawden family has been constructed by W. A. Pilling, Esq., of Colne.

A curious feature of this record is that each male holder of the estate, without exception, was named James. James succeeds James without variation, and even when the first Pilling enters into possession, he is a James Pilling who must adopt the surname of Foulds and henceforth be known as James Pilling Foulds. His younger brother, who followed him, named his eldest son James Pilling, whilst the posthumous son of James P. Foulds was also named James. In all, nine or ten heirs have this Christian name. Usually they married late in life, had few children, and lived to a ripe old age. Hence they seem to have gradually built up a great estate which reached its maximum in the hands of the last of the Foulds's, Miss Mary Foulds, who died in 1817.

Several of the earlier members left Wills which were proved and recorded, and the preludes to these documents show remarkable statements of religious feeling. Thus, "In the name of God, Amen, in the year of our Lord a thousand five hundred four score and four, the 13th of October, be it known unto all men that I James Foulds of Trawden in the County of Lancaster, yeoman, being whole in mind, of good and perfect remembrance, thanks be to Almighty God, sick in body and perceiving that death to all men is most sure, and the hour and time thereof most uncertain, and that many men do die no will by them made, whereby their wife and children be oftentimes unprovided for, their debts unpaid, their friends set at variance and discord, these and many other cases me moving do make this my last Will containing therein my last Testament, the first I do give and bequeath my soul unto Almighty God, my Maker and Redeemer, by the merits of whose death and passion I do believe to be saved, and my body to be buried in the Parish Church or Chapel of Colne." This Will was proved in the Consistory Court at Chester by Jenette his relict on Nov. 11th, 1584. One-third of his estate was settled on his son, James Foulds, one-third on his wife, Jenette, and the remaining third had to be shared by his five daughters, each of whom must have at least £40, which would be a considerable sum in those days. He names fifteen debts owing to him of sums varying from 10/- to £15.

The Will of the James Foulds which was proved in 1704 is equally reverential in its introduction. The executors are his wife Mary, and his son James, and following a peculiar bequest to his brother, John, he leaves to them, "all my personal estate whatsoever which it has pleased God far above my deserts to bestow upon me, equally to be divided betwixt them." To his brother John he bequeathed £10 of current English money, to be paid three full years after his decease, and not before, unless his son James in his discretion shall think fit to pay him before. Also, "John Foulds shall have meat, drink, and lodging at my house at Trawden, he behaving himself soberly and civilly there, and as becomes a brother-in-law to the said Mary, my loving wife, and as an uncle towards my son James, ought or may reasonably be supposed to do, but upon failure on his side by rudeness and incivility to Mary my wife or James my son, it shall be left to their pleasure whether they shall continue meat, drink, and lodging to him." The maiden name of the above wife was Mary Bawden, of Stone Gappe, Lothersdale.

For the James Foulds who died in 1675, an inventory was made of his chattels and debts by Lawrence Brearcliffe, of Burwaynes. In this list there are many kists, quishings (cushions), pewter, silver plate, and venus glasses. Iron gaudlocks and theiles are names of things unknown to us now. The value of a cow was given as £4 to £5. The debts owing to him include one of £30 by Master John Cunliffe, of

Hollins, and another of £2/8/- by Widow Hartley de Lane. In the burial register of Colne Church, this James Foulds is described as, "vir plane generosi," meaning certainly a gentleman.

In the Will of James Foulds, who died in 1725, is mentioned, "several pieces of old gold and silver now in my possession which have been preserved and continued by my ancestors for several years past." This plate goes to his son James, while the plate and linen which belonged to his mother, Mary Foulds, he bequeathed to his daughter, Mary Foulds. His wife was the daughter of Henry Cockcroft, of Mayroyd, Hebden Bridge.

The next James Foulds married Sarah Coates, of Royd House, Kildwick. Her father, Roger Coates, of Kildwick Grange, was a famous Cromwellian magistrate. She brought a large estate in Glusburn, Addingham, and Sutton as her marriage portion. In his Will he instructs his trustiees to sell this portion of his estate, and after making provision for his wife, her sister, and his younger daughter, he leaves his estate, including his ancient mansion house at Trawden, to his elder daughter, Mary Foulds. To his servant, Edward Howarth, he bequeathed £100 for his long and faithful services. His trustees were H. Cockcroft, of Mayroyd, R. Roundell, of Marton, and W. Bawden, of Stonegappe. If his daughters should not reach the age of 21 years, the whole estate would go to Henry Cockcroft, of Mayroyd, his nephew. In 1770 he died a violent death by a self-inflicted thrust with a knife. In later years he was always referred to as Old Squire Foulds.

We then come to the most interesting character of this family and the last of the direct line, Miss Mary Foulds. After her father's death she lived for 47 years, managing her estate with great judgment, and remained unmarried. It is said that Miss Foulds was once asked why she had never married. She replied that no really good man had ever sought her affection, that if she had hung her fortune on the garden gate, no suitor of hers would ever have come forward to the threshhold of her home. Hence she had remained single.

Some of her account books have been carefully treasured, and these show her to have had considerable business ability, and also give many indications of the conditions of life over 100 years ago. She paid annuities to several people. She subscribed annually to the Leeds Infirmary and the Manchester Hospital. Her weekly papers were the

"Leeds Intelligencer," which cost 4d., and the "London Chronicle," which cost 1/3½ weekly. She went to Scaroborough for holidays, and had remittances of £20 or £10 sent to her from her steward at Trawden House. Her steward, whose salary was £21 per annum, kept her accounts in excellent order. Other wages were equally low. A carpenter was paid at the rate of 1/10 per day in 1788, while other men got 1/6 per day. In 1781, when she rebuilt the Red Lion Inn at Colne, a joiner charged 2/3 per day. Once she had to exchange six light half-guineas, and lost three shillings on the transaction. The postage on letters was usually 4½d. or 6d. per letter. In 1797 she paid 10½ guineas to a Mr. Wm. Roberts, of Burnley, as her share of 35 guineas for which he had engaged to find a man and horse to serve in the provisional cavalry, while she also provided three horses.

Her coat-of-arms was a diamond-shaped shield quartered by diagonals into four triangles, two containing a blue cross on a white ground, while the other two bore three laurel leaves on a white ground. Above this shield there was a crest in the form of a crescent. The original Foulds' coat-of-arms carried the three laurel leaves only. The cross was the coat-of-arms of the Coates family of Kildwick, and was adopted when James Foulds married Sarah Coates. The complete heraldic description was :—Arms, Argent, three laurel leaves erect proper ; azure, a cross moline engraved argent ; crest out of a crescent, or, a cross formee sable.

The Foulds' motto was "Thure et Jure," meaning "By religion and right."

Miss Foulds had some difference of opinion with the Vicar of Colne, and would not attend Colne Church, so she drove every Sunday through Wycollar to Haworth and attended divine service at the Parish Church there. The vicar of Haworth, the Rev. James Charnock, was one trustee of her will.

She carefully preserved the heirlooms of silver and gold plate and furniture, and added to the store, so that Trawden Hall was a repository of antique valuables. She gave instructions that at her death a complete inventory should be made and everything of value be preserved in the mansion house as part of the estate. She was keenly interested in her ancestors and relatives, and deplored the fact that she was the last of her race in the direct line. To the wife of one of her tenants, who lived in the farm-house which still stands at Lane Ends, she once expressed her deep grief at this calamity. Her hearer sought to alleviate this distress by telling her that it was common knowledge that William Pilling, of Rings, was her natural half-brother, and therefore her nearest relative. This information led her to adopt his eldest son, James Pilling, as her heir, and to insist that he should adopt the name of James Pilling Foulds.

Her last Will and Testament is a unique document of great length. She had a great desire that men of her family and name should occupy the Hall and keep its treasures intact for a space of five hundred years from the day of her death, and she intailed the estate with this end in view. One proviso was that the person in possession "shall for the space of six successive calendar months in each year, reside, and dwell constantly at or in the said mansion house wherein I now dwell at Trawden. If they refuse, decline, or neglect to do so, the estate shall go to the person or persons next beneficially entitled in remainder."

The second trustee was Thomas Johnson, of Eshton in Craven, gentleman. The trustee had to apply the rent and profits in payment of certain annuities, repairs, and management during the minority of any tenant for life or intail thereof, and use an amount not exceeding £300 a year for the maintenance or education of such minor. The buildings, land, etc., at Oaken Bank were to be held in trust in aid of her personal estate for payment of funeral and testamentary expenses, debts, and legacies. In this way she made every legal provision for the fulfilment of her keen longing to preserve her name and place in the home she loved so well. On the 22nd July, 1817, she died, and was buried in the chancel of Colne Church.

James Pilling, then 10 years old, assumed the name of Foulds, and during his minority was maintained and educated according to the directions of the Will, from the rents and profits of the Trawden estate. He entered into possession of the estate and chattels in August, 1828. He lived the life of a country gentleman, attending to the management of the home farm, riding on horseback frequently to his friends at Eshton, Newall, Broughton, Otley, and Harewood. He attended regularly to his magisterial business at Colne, and was a Justice of the Peace not only in Lancashire, but in company with Captain Atherton, of Alkincoates, and Mr. Green, of Emmott, he qualified in 1843 as a West Riding magistrate. He attended Colne Church and Christ Church until

84

Trawden Church was built, and was very anxious to influence the opinion of Trawden Forest in favour of the Church Rate. He frequently rode with the Craven Harriers, and in 1840 recorded that Mr. Ayre, surgeon, of Colne, was out and had a bad fall, but would not admit that he was hurt. Mrs. Ayre, of Colne, possesses a miniature of Miss Mary Foulds which he gave to her, and which she has allowed me to photograph.

THE FOULDS AND PILLING FAMILIES OF TRAWDEN HALL.

Every New Year's Day Mr. J. P. Foulds systematically began a new diary, but in common with many other diarists, his entries diminished in number and almost ceased before half the year had gone. Many interesting events, however, are recorded with great detail. On April 12th, 1836, he records an agitation against a proposed Church Rate, when he promised to look after Trawden. With this end in view he sent his steward, John Shaw, and Jack at Rings, to go canvassing to Winewall and Wycollar. Two days later there was a meeting at Colne about this rate. After much discussion it was put to the vote, when 148 voted for, and 142 against it. A poll was demanded, and fixed for the 28th of the month. On the 25th, "Wm. Smith, of Trawden, and myself went through the Forest to-day canvassing for the Church Rate, and met with tolerable success at most places, but found that Mr. Midgeley had been before us for the opposite party." On the 28th, "The town of Colne was in a great commotion this morning, Mr. England, the churchwarden, refusing to open the poll for the Church Rate unless each party deposited £20 in his hands as a guarantee for the expenses. The opposite party refused, so there was no poll."

Once, having 45/- available as fines from gamblers, he divided it between the Ranters' Sunday School and the Trawden Church Sunday School.

He took a very keen interest in Church affairs in Trawden from the outset. At the first services at Dog Bottom Cottage, he paid John Berry, of Lanehouse, sixpence per Sunday to assist in the singing. When the first curate, Mr. Pryce, died in 1840, he settled his affairs and provided appropriate funeral arrangements. To the female teachers of the Sunday school he gave ribbons for their bonnets, gloves, and scarves, and to the male teachers, hat bands and gloves. About twenty gentlemen and clergymen who had come to attend the funeral partook of luncheon at Trawden Hall. They started at 2 o'clock, and at Carry Head Lane were met by a number of the respectable inhabitants of Colne who accompanied them to the place of interment at Christ Church.

In February, 1841, the roads to Colne were snowed up for a week. Then they were cut, and the carts for Manchester were able to pass.

It was then a common practice to bleed patients, and he tells how the surgeon on one occasion took from his arm 32 ounces of blood. On another occasion the surgeon bled him, but not so much as he wished, although he was able to sleep after it.

On April 18th, 1845, he laid the foundation stone of the Church of St. Mary the Virgin at Trawden. The proceedings commenced with a procession of teachers and scholars, headed by the brass band, from .he Church School to Trawden House, where they were met by Mr. Foulds, the Revs. John Henderson, H. Stainer, Wm. Hodgson, Wm. Messenger, and other friends. Having re-formed, they walked to the site of the new church, where Mr. Foulds performed the ceremony. and was presented with the customary trowel and mallet.

On the 11th of that month, the funeral of Mr. Walton, of Marsden Hall, took place at Altham, and he writes that such a marked respect he never saw paid to the memory of any deceased; the shops in Colne and Burnley were closed the greater part of the day.

In 1848 he was evidently much surprised to hear the vicar, Mr. Humfrey, preach a written sermon.

At the Winewall "Charity" and on Trawden Rushbearing Sunday he tells how the singers and most of the regular attenders at Trawden Church had gone to other services.

In spite of every advantage that the foresight of Miss Mary Foulds could devise, the life of this last Squire Foulds was a tragic failure. Had he married young and been blessed with a capable wife and children, the record would probably have been pleasanter, but at Trawden Hall, he remained a bachelor. It is difficult now to trace his progress, but he began quite early to accumulate debts, until in 1847 he filed his petition in the County Court with a schedule annexed for the protection of his person against legal process. The estate should then have become vested in the Clerk of the County Court, but proceedings were stayed because of a private arrangement for his creditors to collect all revenues and to pay him £200 per year so long as he observed the conditions of Miss Foulds' Will, i.e., to reside at Trawden Hall and to keep the heirlooms, and furniture and other effects in good repair, order and condition, the creditors then granting to him full liberty of action.

In July, 1859, however, his younger brother, William Pilling, claimed the right to enter into possession of the Trawden Estate as tenant in tail male, and to evict James Pilling Foulds; who had caused a forfeiture of the estate and interests of himself and his issue by his non-residence at the mansion house at Trawden.

This forfeiture was at first disputed by the creditors and others entitled to the benefit of the encumbrances on the life estate of J. P. Foulds. Then William Pilling caused a Bill of Complaint to be prepared against James P. Foulds, and was about to commence litigation when an amicable arrangement was effected between William Pilling and the creditors, the trustees agreeing to vest the legal estate in William Pilling. A deed for the disentailment was forthwith prepared and executed by all interested parties. The creditors agreed to forbear to dispute the forfeiture by James P. Foulds, and William Pilling agreed to make a grant of an annuity of £500 yearly for the term of the natural life of James P. Foulds.

This concession by William Pilling may perhaps be better appreciated when it is considered that he was a very poor man with a very large family. From such a condition, to enter into undisturbed possession of the Trawden Estate, was sufficient to test a man's character, even though the possibility had always been kept in mind.

He enjoyed his inheritance for only seven years, and during this period frequently corresponded with his elder brother, who was living in the Isle of Man, and sent him presents.

William Pilling was elected Vice-Chairman of the Trawden Local Board from its formation in 1863, and served on it until his death in 1867. In the next following meeting the members desired to record his death in the minutes, "whom," they said, "we lament for the loss which the Board will sustain by losing one of its most useful members " Few residents of Trawden Hall can have had such a chequered career. He knew from his earliest years the possibility of inheriting great wealth, and was educated with that end in view, yet for nearly forty years he had a ceaseless struggle for bare existence. His action in disentailing the estate, although not in keeping with the wishes of Miss Mary Foulds, shows his anxiety to distribute his wealth among his children rather than favour the heir. The result was to make many smaller estates, and the heir, James Pilling, did not long retain Trawden Hall in his possession.

No inventory or schedule of the possessions of Miss Foulds in Trawden Hall was ever made or taken, according to her directions, or at any rate no one was ever able to discover any, or that James P. Foulds gave any receipt for such chattels. The valuable heirlooms were distributed, and many pieces of plate engraved with the Foulds' coat of arms are still in the possession of the several descendants of the Pillings.

James P. Foulds never returned to Trawden, but remained at Douglas in the Isle of Man. In 1861 he married, and in 1864 he died, leaving a widow surviving and enciente with a male child, who was afterwards called James Henry D'Arcy Foulds. This provided another source of litigation, and the surviving trustee, Thomas Mason Johnson, of Eshton Hall, filed a Bill of Complaint in the Court of Chancery. The residuary personal estate of Miss Mary Foulds had accumulated to the value of £9,000, and this was claimed by the younger brothers and sisters of William Pilling, of Rings, on the one hand, and for the entire and exclusive benefit of James Henry D'Arcy Foulds on the other. Hence the aid and authority of the Court of Chancery was invoked to decide between the claims of the contending parties.

In the history of the Foulds and Pillings we have incident and tragedy rarely surpassed in the pages of romance. Perhaps some day a writer of ability will do justice to the thoughts and hopes of that wonderful lady, Miss Mary Foulds, and thus keep her memory green. Her coat of arms formed part of a stained-glass window in the dining room of Trawden Hall, and used to fire my boyish imagination, as I read under it, the inscription, "Mary Foulds, obiit 1817," not knowing at that time what history she had made.

The last James Pilling sold the home of his ancestors to William Marsden, Esq., cotton manufacturer, who occupied it for some years, after which it passed into the possession of the present owner, John Hopkinson, Esq. By that time it had become very dilapidated, and from a series of photographs, taken by Mr. Spivey, architect, before its demolition, it possessed few remarkable features of architectural interest.

One can therefore understand the decision of the owner to build a new modern mansion on the old site with all the advantages of surroundings that only age can give.

OTHER LOCAL FAMILIES.

THE MIDGELEY FAMILY OF STUNSTEAD HALL IN WINEWALL.

Stunstead Hall, on the ridge facing Trawden Hall, was the home of the Midgeleys from 1694, when Robert Midgeley bought it from James Driver, until 1869, when the last male survivor died. They were people of considerable importance and wealth as is shown by their bequests and legacies. The last William Midgeley was Chairman of the Trawden Local Board from its formation in 1863 until his death in 1869. He was the last of the old mill masters who were responsible for the parish corn mill, and as such he claimed rent for it. He built "the streets" in the lower part of Trawden, and the Upper Stunstead Laithe, on which until quite recently there were gargoyles which represented his wife and his only son. His son died young from an attack of smallpox during one of those frequently recurring epidemics which used to scar a large propor-tion of the inhabitants. It may be of interest to learn that the masons employed on the above structure were paid at the rate of two shillings per day, while the sculptor, the highest paid man of all, got half-a-crown per day.

THE DRIVERS OF WINEWALL.

The family of Driver is a very ancient one. Stunstead Hall was probably built by one of the Drivers. The oldest Latin deed held by the present owner, Joseph Bannister, Esq., shows that James Driver owned it in 1675. In an Inquisition made by a Commission in 1662, the only Driver in the Forest was John Driver, of Stunstead, who was one of the largest landowners in Winewall, being rated at £1/8/11½. This copyhold rental was paid by John Driver in 1608, and by other members as far back as 1526. This family probably took up the land at Stun-stead at the disafforestation in 1507, as two years later, in 1509, there is a complaint recorded in the Court Rolls against Geoffrey Driver and another in a plea of trespass, and for detention of a parcel of land lying "in le Fens in Trawden," the herbage whereof they had consumed for two years, that is, since the disafforestation.

In the Court Rolls for 1541 there is a curious entry, which throws light on a practice in law which, to us, is very strange. In that year

John Driver complained against James Driver in a plea of £2/13/4, being the substance of the goods of his child's portion in arrears. Defendant appeared and claimed "wager of law," and this was granted. Wager of law was used in action for debt, and for goods left with or lent to another person. It was held that the defendant might have paid privately, or have obtained no receipt, or the witnesses might be dead, or in other ways be unavailable. The law then allowed the defendant the right to take oath, along with other persons called compurgators, that he did not owe the money. In this case of Driver v. Driver, the defendant James, appeared before the Court with eleven compurgators, and they swore the debt was not owing, or, in legal phraseology, he "did wage his law." It was accepted by the Court as a perfect clearance for him, and the plaintiff was at the mercy of the Court.

The family of Driver is one of the most ancient in the township of Colne. William le Driver appears in the taxation list of 1333, and Thomas Driver in the list of Colne tenants in 1443. John Driver was a frequent juror at the Colne Halmot Court from 1500 onwards. It therefore appears that the family sprang from Colne, and secured a settlement in Trawden Forest when it was thrown open to public ownership. They were of some importance, as is shown by members of the family occupying the position of Greave of the Forest, etc. In the reigns of the Tudor monarchs the Driver family appear as contributing to the various subsidies on account of their lands, but vanish in the reigns of Elizabeth and of Charles I., from which it is probable that they had removed from Colne and were established in Winewall. As the name Stunstead does not appear before 1662, they probably built that house not long before that date. They have always formed an important section of the Winewall hamlet up to the present time.

THE HARTLEYS.

The Hartleys were among the earliest settlers in each division of the Forest, and for a long time were the most important tenants. It is impossible, however, to construct their ancestral tree with its numerous branches, because no particular family residences can be assigned to them for any considerable period.

Piers Hartley settled in Wycollar previous to 1507, and built Wycollar Hall in 1550.

Sir William P. Hartley, whose father was a Trawden man, has

frequently shown his interest in the village by generously helping the Primitive Methodists there.

There are still many members of the Hartley family, but the last to come prominently before the public and earn the deep gratitude of Trawden people are Mr. and Mrs. Stephen Hartley, of Pendle View, Winewall. Early in 1921 the Trawden Urban District Council were anxious to provide a recreation ground and playing fields for the district. The most appropriate site was the Jubilee Meadow, which occupies a very central position. A sub-committee appointed to interview Mr. and Mrs. Hartley, with regard to the purchase of this meadow, learnt that they had already agreed to sell the meadow to Mr. Thornton and Mr. R. H. Bannister, who in turn had re-sold it at a profit to Councillor S. Howard, Chairman of the Urban District Council. Mr. and Mrs. Hartley generously offered to give the land to the Urban District Council, provided that they could be relieved from their obligations with the other gentlemen concerned, on the conditions that it should be preserved and kept in good repair by the Council, and be considered as a memorial to the great-hearted lads of the district who made the Supreme Sacrifice in the War.

Councillor Howard persuaded Messrs. Thornton and Bannister to release both Mr. and Mrs. Hartley and himself in these transactions, and on their doing so gave £100, the proposed profits of the re-sale, towards the cost of erection of conveniences and shelters on the recreation ground.

Councillor T. Robinson, the life tenant of Well Head Farm, of which Jubilee Meadow is a portion, very generously offered to give up possession to the Council at once, and the land was immediately utilised by the villagers.

THE BANNISTERS.

My own ancestors have lived in Trawden for about two centuries and during that time have taken an active part in the social and public life. They came to Trawden from Park Hill, Barrowford, where they had lived for many generations. The original house at Park Hill was erected before 1460, and the Colne Parish Church Registers, commencing in 1599, contain many entries of the baptisms, marriages, and deaths of members of the Park Hill Bannister family.

The present house at Park Hill was built in 1661, but as the family fortunes declined it came into possession of Mr. John Swingle-hurst. The Park Hill Bannisters had long owned the northern choir of Colne Parish Church, which was formerly called the Bannister or Park Hill Chancel or Choir. Much strife and litigation resulted in order to decide whether the rights to this choir should be owned by the Bannisters, then in Trawden, or by Mr. Swinglehurst, of Park Hill. By a decree of the Consistory Court of Chester made in 1743 a settlement was made by which the rights to this choir were divided between the two disputants, Mr. Swinglehurst obtaining the right to have reserved for his sole use the northern moiety and the four pews therein, while Mr. Henry Bannister, of Trawden, and his successors, owners of the other moiety, had the sole right to bury his and their dead under the northern moiety, when and as occasion should require, replacing immediately after the interment of any "corps" there, the seats taken up on the occasion.

The grandson of Henry Bannister was "Old" John Bannister, of Nichol House, my great-grandfather, who in 1831 advertised for sale, "the spacious, substantial, dry, comfortable and well situated pew with a boarded floor, then tenanted by Mrs. George Carr, and containing ample room for eight adults or grown-up persons. Also the right of sepulture or burial throughout the whole of the ground of the chancel, called Bannister's Chancel, on the north side of the greatest chancel, without payment of the usual fees for breaking the earth for vaults or graves, as is the custom in the other chancels and body of the church."

No sale took place, but pew rent was paid to my ancestors during the next forty years, until the present system replaced these ancient family rights.

The historian, Baines, says that the Bannister family of Park Hill, Barrowford, was founded by the Bannisters of Banke Hall and Altham. Both were important county families, some members of which occupied high positions. Sir Thomas Bannister, of Banke Hall, was a Knight of the Garter in 1375, while his descendant, Christopher Bannister, who died in 1649, had been vice-chancellor, recorder, attorney general, and baron of the Exchequer of Lancashire.

The last heiress of the Bannister family of Altham married Ambrose Walton, of Marsden Hall. Her grandson, Benastre Walton, built Walton Spire near Shelfield, and gave the land on which the

Colne Cloth Hall was built. He died without issue, the last Walton of Marsden Hall.

The genealogies of these families are given in great detail in the various histories and heraldry records. The several branches in Lancashire of Bannisters, or Banastres, have their descent recorded from a Robert Banastre, a knight of William the Conqueror, whose name is on the roll of Battle Abbey in 1066. He was granted lands at Prestatyn, North Wales, and also became feudal baron of Makerfield in Lancashire. One of his descendants in 1130 became Lord of Walton le Dale near Preston. The last heiress of this line married John de Langton who succeeded to the baronship of Newton and lordship of Walton. The Bannisters of Darwin Hall or Bannister Hall traced their descent from the same source.

The names of Blackburn, Holgate, Tatham, Pickles, Mitchell, Tillotson, Shackleton, Shuttleworth, and Emmott have long been owned by residents in the Forest, but records of these families are not available.

CHAPTER XIII.

PUBLIC INSTITUTIONS.

THE TRAWDEN GAS AND WATER COMPANY, LTD.

Until 1878 water for domestic purposes was obtained from wells, some of which had a great reputation. The old "Bold Venture Well" at the bottom of Church Street, near the old Corn Mill, and the Well Head Spring in Winewall, supplied water which was more renowned for its purity and goodness than any modern filtered water.

In that year the Trawden Gas and Water Company, Ltd., was formed, with a capital of £2,000, to construct waterworks and supply water within the township and to manufacture, sell, let, or supply all articles connected with the supply of water. Also to make, store, and supply gas within the township, and to manufacture, sell, provide, supply, and deal in coke, coal, tar, pitch, asphaltum, ammoniacal liquor, and all other products or residum of any materials employed in the manufacture of gas, and all articles connected with the supply of gas. Also to purchase or take gas or water or both in bulk from any sanitary authority, corporation, company, or person.

The first subscribers and directors were Blackburn Holgate, mason; Robert Barritt, engine-tenter; Ellis Blackburn, coal miner; John Bannister, manufacturer; William Marsden, manufacturer; George Sowerby, schoolmaster; Thomas Bannister, grocer.

Supplies of water were obtained from springs at Naze End, at Wanlass Farm, and at Oakenbank Farm, Hoyle. The Urban District Council at a later date bought out the Company, and as the demand increased, they obtained a plentiful supply from Boulsworth Hill, near Lumb Laithe Farm. This spring, together with the Naze End spring, now supply the village.

The Company never built a gas plant nor took over the existing plants. The early power-loom cotton manufacturers had been quick to see the advantages of coal-gas lighting, and coal-gas plants were erected and worked for many years at Hollin Hall Mill, Lane House Mill, Pave Shed, and at Messrs. Critchleys Mill, Cottontree. Such small plants were not economical, and they were abandoned when a much better and cheaper supply of coal gas was offered from Colne.

THE LITERARY INSTITUTE.

There have been several Mechanics' Institutes and Social Clubs, but in 1879 there was a movement to provide the village with something more than a social club, with a building that would be an educational centre. A company, The Trawden Literary Institute, Ltd., was formed, with the following objects :—The formation, building, furnishing and carrying on of a Literary Institute in Trawden ; the letting or using from time to time of such a building or any parts thereof, for concerts, lectures, meetings of friendly societies or other similar purposes ; the establishment of a library in connection with such institute ; the purchase and circulation of sound and wholesome literature of a religious and secular nature ; the lending out and disposal of the same ; the purchase of a plot of land, and of any other real or personal property.

The first subscribers were Edward Bannister, weaver ; John Pickles, twister ; Charles Blackburn, mason ; Thomas Hartley, over-looker ; William Bracewell, weaver ; Hartley Ellis, weaver ; William Chadwick, butcher.

The first trustees were Hartley Bannister, tailor ; James Heap, weaver ; James Pickles, weaver ; and William Pickles, weaver.

The company was formed with a capital of £1,000, and an institute was built in Lane House, but it never became the successful educational centre for the village that its promoters had desired. It most nearly approached this ideal during the years 1892 to 1896, when very successful advanced science and mathematical classes, under the Science and Art Department, were conducted there by the present Dr. A. Wilmore. No classes of this character have been attempted since he left the village. The Literary Institute is now owned by and forms the offices of the Urban District Council.

THE TRAWDEN BRASS BAND.

During the latter half of the last century, when brass bands were very much more appreciated than they are at the present time, the Trawden Band was said to be second to none in the North of England. This is no vain boast, because on several occasions, in open contest, they were placed equal with or above the famous bands of Besses o' th' Barn, Black Dyke, Kingston Mills, and so on.

It was to celebrate one of their many successes, when they had

95

secured the first prize in open contest at Nelson, that the late Mr. W. B. White, of Colne, wrote his poem about Grand Old Trawden.

The first brass band was called the Upper Town Band, and was formed about 1840-1850. Previous to this there had been a reed band, which took part in the celebrations of the coronation of Queen Victoria, but it was disbanded soon afterwards. Shortly before 1850 another brass band was organised at Trawden Hill, with Mr. Harrison Whittaker as conductor. Both bands joined for an open air soiree, which had been promoted by the Mechanics' Institute of Trawden Hill, and which was a very famous local event, attracting all the most prominent men in the district. Not long afterwards the Upper Town Band was disbanded, while the other band developed into the famous Trawden Brass Band. About 1862 the Band secured a lease of the White House, which was their home for over twenty years.

The first contest in which they took part was at Skipton in 1864, but no prize was then secured. In the following year, however, J. Lord, of Bacup, was appointed professional teacher, and reward attended the efforts of the performers, for at the Waterfoot contest they received the third prize and a Higham Soprano Cornet. Later in the same year, at the Burnley contest, they carried off the first prize of £25, and an E flat bombardon. Local pride rose high with the winning of these two prizes, and to mark the events a grand parade was held. Mr. John Dixon headed the procession on horseback; then came the two prize instruments, borne aloft on a wooden framework, with the band following as they marched round the village.

In 1863 the Band had a memorable engagement at Burnley on the occasion of the festivities arranged to celebrate the marriage of His Late Majesty, King Edward VII., who was then Prince of Wales.

In 1867, at the Burnley Agricultural Society's Contest, they won the third prize. Also in a contest for a cornet solo, with band accompaniments, Mr. Harrison Whittaker, of Trawden Band, and Mr. J. Turner, of Keighley Band, were selected to re-play, and the Trawden conductor was awarded the trophy, a silver-plated B flat cornet, by F. Besson, value £13/13/-.

Up to that time there was no uniform, but in that year a public subscription was opened for this purpose, and in this way over £26 was raised towards £87/2/-, the cost of a set of uniforms. The playing of Christmas Carols and selections at that festive tide then realised about £16 to £18.

In 1868 a Brass Band Contest was promoted at Trawden, and for about twenty years was one of the most striking annual events. These contests were very popular, attracting bands from all parts of the country. On one occasion twenty-four bands entered, and all turned up. At the 1871 contest the gate money amounted to over £56, while on several other occasions it exceeded £50.

A first prize of £25 was won at the Middleton contest in 1869.

The year 1875 was the most successful as regards successes at contests. From June to September they secured seven prizes, as follows :—Linthwaite, 2nd prize ; Bury, 2nd prize and a baritone ; Golcar, 2nd prize ; Hollingworth Lake, 2nd prize ; Whitehaven, 1st prize and a silver cup ; Middleton, 2nd prize ; and Barrow, 1st prize.

They had long runs of annual engagements at Rawtenstall, Facit, Bolton-by-Bowland, and Downham, the one at Facit extending for over thirty years.

Mr. J. Gladney, of Manchester, became professional teacher to the Band in 1876, and in 1879 this position was given to Mr. Alex. Owen, of Manchester, and retained by him for over twenty years.

On the Whit-Monday of 1881 the Band played for a scholars' procession at Accrington in the morning, and in the afternoon of the same day competed in the contest at Stanley Park, Liverpool, winning the second prize, and on that occasion beating Besses o' th' Barn Band. They remained at this park on the three following days, and on the Friday fulfilled their annual Facit engagement. The prize money and fees for that week amounted to the record sum of £89.

At the Hawes contest in 1896 the fourth and fifth prizes were divided between the Trawden and Kingston Mills Bands.

Many other prizes were won, but the above summary will indicate the eminence of the Band in the latter part of the last century.

For about forty years Mr. H. Whittaker was conductor, being succeeded by Messrs. W. H. Wadsworth, J. Hartley, W. Whittaker, C. Holgate, and A. Broadhead. The latter bandmaster led the way to a great revival of interest and success, with 1903 as a great record year of successes. In that year the Band competed at 10 contests and won 14 prizes, these being as follows :—Colne, 2nd prize both for march and for selection, and medal for the best soloist, Mr. C. Birtwistle; Whitworth, 2nd prize for march; Earby, 1st prize for both march and selection; Elslack, 1st prize for march, 2nd prize for selection; Nelson, 2nd prize for march, 4th prize for selection; Barnoldswick, 1st prize for march and 1st prize for chorus; Cornholme, 2nd prize both for march and chorus; Burnley, 2nd prize for selection, medal for best euphonium player, to Mr. A. Broadhead, and medal for best trombone player, to Mr. H. Pickles. In 1904 a grand bazaar was held to raise funds for clearing the debt on the Band premises at Clogg Heads. From the booklet compiled on that occasion by my brother, Hartley Bannister, I am indebted for the above account.

CHAPTER XIV.

LOCAL GOVERNMENT.

While the district was only a deer forest or chace there was little need for any system of local government, and a description has already been given of the methods of keeping order among the earliest settlers. An Inquisition or Enquiry was held by a jury of the principal inhabitants, at the head of whom was the Greave. Other officials were appointed for special duties, and fines were laid on any of the inhabitants who disregarded the ancient customs.

In those far distant times the cattle and sheep were driven daily from the homesteads and folds to the common pasture, until the evening, when they were driven home again. The depredations of the wolves among the flocks and herds, and of the deer, among the cornfields, were grievous, and could only be avoided by constant watch kept in turn by the husbandmen. These conditions meant common life, common pasturage among the woods or near the moor, a common wood, a common mill, a common turbary, and so on. The road to these places was the common way. From such conditions of life have come the words, "Commons, Commonwealth, House of Commons."

The old Halmot Court is still in existence, although many of its former duties and powers have long since fallen into abeyance.

In the 18th century, township meetings were held, either in the Winewall Chapel, or in the Rock Inn, Trawden. Their duties seem to have been to assess the rates, to keep the highways in proper condition and to provide for the poor. From a book kindly lent me by H. Holgate, Esq., architect, of Colne, some details of interest have been gleaned for the period 1790 to 1862.

At a meeting of the principal inhabitants of the Forest of Trawden in 1798, it was resolved that two orphan girls should be bound apprentices by indenture, one to Robert Hartley, of Buttock Laithe, and the other to Thomas Whittaker, of Parson Lee, till they attained the respective ages of 21 years. The former girl apparently did not give satisfactory service, because in the following year £10 was received from Robert Hartley, being a fine incurred by refusing to accept the apprentice who had been put out in 1798 by rotation. The fine was placed in the receipts and applied to the use of the poor of the township.

In the Trawden Hall deeds there is a curious note regarding the above Robert Hartley. In giving evidence on a question of boundaries in 1840, this farmer, then 79 years old, said that he went to the farm "43 years ago, namely, in the spring of the year next before the year of scarcity commonly known as the barley year."

Allowances were made, "to Christopher Hartley of one and six-pence a week, and to blind James, for the present, six shillings."

In 1799, Thomas Heaton succeeding Jonas Horsfall as Constable for the Forest of Trawden, took into his possession a set of iron weights, one each of 1, 2, 4, 7, 14, 28, and 56 lbs., with bank and scales.

In the Highways Account for 1814-15, the rate was sixpence in the pound, and the larger ratepayers contributed their quota partly by cash and partly by work. The rates realised £47/10/3. The surveyor was paid 2/6 per day for the number of days, 283, actually worked. In 1838, the total rates were £42/8/1½. The hire of a horse and cart per day was then 4/6.

During the year ending March, 1839, a bridge had been built at a cost of £70, and the cost of making the road to the bridge was £45/2/1½. This was probably the Dogbottom Bridge. The rates collected for that year amounted to £132/3/2½.

In 1844, John Harrison, of Winewall; John Hartley, of Wycollar; and Henry Hindle, of Trawden, were appointed road surveyors at a salary of £10 per year each, to work two days a week with the men through the whole year, and collect the highway rates also. The total length of highways in the three hamlets was 12 miles 1142 yards.

THE TRAWDEN LOCAL. BOARD.

The Local Board was formed in 1863, and consisted of William Midgeley, chairman; William Pilling, vice-chairman; Henry Tatham, William Wilkinson, Joseph Wallbank, Thomas Shaw, John Hartley, William Pickles, and William Heaton. In the following year, Thomas Bannister was appointed Clerk to the Board, and John Tatham, surveyor, at a salary of £6 yearly, with power to engage a foreman under him at 2/6 per day, and men labourers at 2/- per day. The nuisance inspector received 5/- per annum.

Gravel from the water courses was used as road metal at first, and the loose sand on the road on Lancashire Moor and other places was sold to John Pilling, of the Primet Bridge Foundry, for 6d. per cartload.

In 1868 a proposal was carried for the construction of a water-works and gas supply, and for a special district which would benefit by it to be separately assessed and rated for general improvements. Although plans and estimates were prepared, the resolution was re-scinded in the following year. In 1868, the farmer at Alderbarrow sent in a request to the Board that a pinfold be made, thereby showing a desire for an old custom that had been allowed to lapse.

From 1866 to 1873, the proceedings of the Board were frequently very animated, because in the former year, Mr. Joseph Bannister pro-posed that a New Road be made from Trawden to Cotton Tree for the benefit of the township. The land required was given by the owners. In 1868, Mr. William Burr was first mentioned as solicitor to the Board, being appointed Clerk to the Board two years later, and members of his firm have occupied this position ever since.

The twelve tenders submitted for the construction of the New Road varied from £4,300 to £2,130, three of these being from Winewall or Trawden men. The lowest tender, being that of William Clough, of Bacup, was accepted. The work was not carried out to the satisfaction of the engineer, so Mr. Clough was dismissed, and one of his sureties continued the work by contract.

In 1870 Mr. Joseph Bannister offered his gratuitous services as Clerk of Works to the New Road, and they were accepted with thanks.

About this time Richard Hartley, of Wycollar, and Edward James Taylor, of Colne, read a protest against the expenditure on the New Road, and also against the Board, for calling upon the whole township to contribute by Rate, instead of calling on those who were specially benefited by such road. These gentlemen, active in opposition, and frequently in a minority of two, being in this case supported by many ratepayers, sent a Memorial to the Home Secretary. As a result there was a Local Government Board enquiry in September, 1870, from which the Local Board emerged with high compliments from the Inspector for their foresight and good business management.

In his Report he describes how the Winewall and Wycollar

hamlets before the adoption of the Local Government Act in 1860 had repaired their own roads, ratione tenure, or by apportionment. The hamlet of Trawden had repaired its own roads out of a Highway Rate collected from its own property only. After 1860, all the roads were repaired out of the Highway Rate until the Board was advised that it was illegal, upon which notice was given to the hamlets of Winewall and Wycollar to repair their roads by apportionment as before. The two hamlets refused to do this, so legal proceedings were commenced, but the Local Board intimated their willingness to assist those liable to repair their roads, ratione tenure, in any course they might be advised to take and also to have the expenses incurred paid out of a General District Rate.

The memorialists had alleged that the New Road would not be of any advantage except to a very small proportion of the property in the district, that it was promoted only by owners of property along its line, and not by the ratepayers generally. The opposition, however, did not arise until the New Road was very nearly completed.

The original estimate of its cost was £3,690, but the cost had been very much less, so that the charge of extravagance was unfounded, the greatest economy having been exercised in all instances. Hence the memorialists failed to prove their charges. The Report suggested that help should be given to release the two hamlets from their liability to repair highways, and concluded by declaring that the New Road must materially tend to improve the whole district as giving facilities to traffic and opening out land for mills and other building purposes, which would otherwise have remained purely agricultural.

The claims of the contractor, Mr. Clough, led to a trial at the Liverpool Assizes, from whence the Arbitrator transferred the discussion to London. A majority of the Board considered that this litigation was owing largely to the conduct of Messrs. Hartley and Taylor, and recorded their disapproval of such conduct.

In 1872-3 several Winewall tenants refused to repair their portion of highway, and were prosecuted, but in the latter year application was made that Winewall be made a township highway. The working surveyor's wages was then 3/6 per day.

In 1874 it was resolved, "that the Board desires to express its deep sorrow for the death of the late Mr. Thomas Shaw, one of its oldest members, one who has since the first constitution of the Board laboured indefatigably to promote its best interest and those of the township and district, whose judgment and unwearied industry have been of the greatest possible use to the ratepayers, and that this resolution be communicated to the family of the deceased, with whom this Board heartily sympathises under their heavy bereavement.''

In the next year the Board expressed its deep sorrow for the death of the late Christopher Bridge, the Chairman of the Board.

In 1876 the Clerk was instructed to enquire if the Court Rolls or other document at Clitheroe Castle would show the grant of a spring of water by the Duke of Buccleuch to the township of Trawden, such spring being called Bold Venture, and running near the old Corn Mill, and in the event of the reply being satisfactory that a deputation wait upon Messrs. Critchley and Co. and ascertain if they would be willing to exchange one of their springs for that to which the Board believe they have a title.

More recent events are within the memory of many people now living, and must wait description by some future writer.

In 1894 the Local Board became an Urban District Council, and recent events up to the present year show that Trawden Forest has never lacked men who would gladly give their best services for the welfare of their fellow men and for future posterity.

CHAPTER XV.

In an earlier chapter it was shown that the name Forest or Chase did not always signify an area of trees, but a wide expanse over which the deer or other wild animals roamed and were hunted. It is doubtful whether the higher pastures and the moorlands were ever forested, but there is no doubt that the lower lands and river valleys were much more thickly wooded than they are now.

The last forest patch to disappear was the Carry Heys Wood, which extended to what is still called the Wood Bottoms at Cotton Tree. The trees in this wood were cut down about 1860-1870.

A survey book of Forests on the Trawden Hall Estate, made in 1801, shows that in 16 woods, the first nine of which were in Trawden Forest, each tree was numbered, described, and valued, and in the case of oak trees, the bark also had a market value, because it was useful for tanning leather. The small trees were described as cyphers, and were not valued.

In the Dogbottom Wood, stretching from where the Primitive Methodist Chapel now stands to the river and beyond Job Lane, there were 241 trees and 99 cyphers, including 41 ash, 176 oak, 11 elm, and 5 alder trees. This wood has entirely disappeared. At Whitelee Carr above the old Corn Mill there were 254 trees and 51 cyphers, including 126 ash and 116 oak trees. At Rings Wood, including Carry Heys Wood and Hell Hole Wood, opposite the present Gladstone Terrace, there were 974 trees and 228 cyphers, among which were 221 ash, 658 oak, and 36 plane trees. The plantation below Winewall Bridge had 268 trees, with a majority of plane trees. At Widow Catlow's, at Hoyle, there were three ash trees; at Well Head Farm, 36 trees and 9 cyphers; and at Hartley Laycock's Farm at Winewall, 20 trees. The plantation near Trawden Hall contained 53 trees and 13 cyphers, most of which were described as "dale" trees. Backside Farm possessed 55 trees and 3 cyphers.

Outside Trawden Forest the High Rideough Farm at Thursden had 27 trees and 4 cyphers; Swindon Farm, 419 trees and 16 cyphers; Farther Lee Farm, 90 trees and 12 cyphers; Near Lee Farm, 4 trees; Lob Common, 8 trees. At the Royd House Farm there were 180 trees and 20 cyphers, and below Sutton Mill 58 trees and 92 cyphers.

In the Trawden Forest portion there were 1,904 trees and 403 cyphers, while on the whole estate there were 3,237 trees and 547 cyphers, the value of wood and bark being then estimated at £896/15/-.

It is much to be regretted that so little interest has been taken in forestry, not only in Trawden, but in all the neighbouring districts, that the extensive woods have been destroyed and few trees planted to replace them. May the day soon come when men will take pride in planting trees, although only their descendants may enjoy them. Then again will the Trawden Valley become beautiful with the leafy foliage and majestic splendour that only well developed trees can give to the landscape.

Even now the wide expanse of moorland, impressive in the cold dark days of winter, and exhilarating in the heat of summer, will always provide the most bracing air of all the country side, and be ever waiting to inspire lofty thoughts and to give health and freshness to the jaded town dweller.

_____

The Forest will never lack charm to the stranger, and proud is he who can claim it as his birthplace. It has given to the neighbouring towns many of the most prominent inhabitants both in industrial and professional circles. It is very tempting to make much of their influence in the development of "Bonnie Colne," but I refrain. Comparatively few in number, they are like leaven which can leaven the whole lump.

The brief record herein attempted is a history quite typical but probably not surpassed in interest or romance by that of any village in North-East Lancashire. I trust I have not claimed undue merit for my native village. To all who have helped me in the collection of material I tender again my deepest thanks, and sincerely hope that I have not in any degree given offence to people now living.

My chief aims in compiling these Annals have been to win respect from the stranger, to develop local pride, and to encourage some young people to equal or surpass their ancestors in building up a worthy record. Only by sojourning for many years in the wilderness of a great city can one fully appreciate the value and charm of life in a country village, where there is a society complete in miniature, exhibiting all the strength and frailty, the humour and pathos of our race. It is a great asset to have been reared in a village near the hills.

As a field for the future novelist Trawden Forest is rich in opportunities. Stories about the buried kist of gold, the poaching on Boulsworth both by solitary game hunters, or by groups of night hunters, the tragic incidents of the Cotton Famine, the remarkable religious revivals, the romance of Trawden Hall, the many eccentric characters, the successful struggles of ambitious men, all provide topics now waiting for the imaginative writer, and when he comes, the Forest may well win a place in literature comparable with Drumtochty, Thrums, or any other famous village. Poet and novelist can make word pictures of scenery and natural phenomena, but to arouse the highest emotions, the place must be made the home of good men, rich in noble thoughts and deeds, gentlemen in truth even though they are never known to the greater world, nor rise to eminence in their own little world. To the many such men who now live and have lived in Trawden Forest, I conclude my notes by hoping that this record has won their appreciation.

(The End.)